MAKING & DECORATING PICTURE FRAMES

JANET BRIDGE

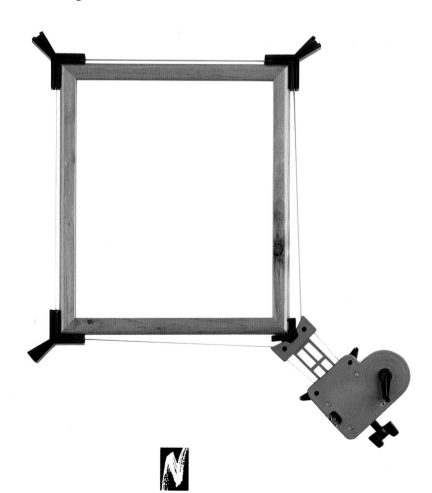

NORTH LIGHT BOOKS

Cincinnati, Ohio

First Published in North America
in 1996 by North Light Books, an imprint of F & W Publications, Inc.,
1507 Dana Avenue,
Cincinnati, Ohio 45207
1-800/289-0963

© Salamander Books, 1996

ISBN 0-89134-739-9

1 3 5 7 9 8 6 4 2

Managing Editor: Joanna Smith
Art Editor: John Heritage
Photographer: Simon Butcher
Photographer's Assistant: Giles Stokoe
Stylist: Janet Bridge
Original Design Concept: Town Group Consultancy
Color Separation: Pixel Tech Pte Ltd, Singapore
Printed in China

CONTENTS

INTRODUCTION

If you are anything like me, you probably have drawers full of posters and prints from places visited, which you intended to frame when you returned home. But what seems to start out as an inexpensive memento of an enjoyable holiday can become unacceptably costly when you have it framed professionally. This can also apply when you are decorating your home or office. An inexpensive but impressive piece of artwork can enhance a wall but with the cost of framing, it becomes a questionable luxury. Even ready made frames can be expensive and with the limited choice available, it is often impossible to find something that really suits the picture you are framing.

This book shows you how to make your own frames, including the basic techniques of making a simple frame right from the initial measurements, through cutting the moulding, mount and glass to the final assembly of the finished frame. It is not as difficult as you may think and you don't need specialist tools; those required are easily available.

As well as basic frame making, there are sections on decorating frames, from beautiful paint finishes, to innovative craft ideas for unusual and exciting frames and mounts. You will also find advice on how to select the best frame for your picture, and the practical details of framing all sorts of pictures such as oils, photographs and water colours.

With the information and advice at hand, and plenty of photographs to illustrate each section, I hope this book inspires and gives you the confidence to undertake your own framing at home. Whether you are making a frame from scratch or decorating an existing one, you will discover the pleasure and satisfaction of producing something that is unique and perfect for you.

Janet Bridge

CHAPTER ONE

CHOOSING
A STYLE

Other than ensuring a piece of artwork is framed in the right manner technically, the only consideration when choosing a framing style is that it enhances rather than detracts from the picture. The frame and the mount (if used) should be chosen to complement the style and colour and create a complete visual image. To help you make this choice, this section includes tips on how to select frames, choosing a framing style, and the correct way to frame oils, water colours, photographs and so on. There are also photographs of framed works to inspire and help you make the right decision.

CHOOSING A STYLE

Pictures are framed for both aesthetic and practical reasons. A frame forms a boundary that limits the extent of the picture; it stops the eye wandering from the picture into the room beyond, and its shape gives purpose and balance to the composition of the work. It also serves to protect the work, not only while hanging on a wall, but also while being moved.

As a general rule, the frame, whilst being obvious, should not detract from the picture but rather complement and enhance it. Correct framing may be subtle and not instantly obvious, yet it will serve to bring admiration from the viewer; incorrect framing may cause the viewer to wince. The balance, colour, size or style of the frame and mount (if used) is then doing nothing for the picture. The frame should interact with the picture, not compete with it. The beauty of making your own frames is that the mood of the frame can be more easily matched to the mood of the picture. Different frames work for different pictures and there are no hard and fast rules, but make sure you consider different styles before you choose one. There are many from which to choose and you should ask yourself a number of questions before making a decision.

For instance, will the picture benefit from a modern or antique effect frame? Should it be ornate or does the picture need a plain frame? How big should the frame be and does the picture need a mount? If so, what colour should the mount be? You may find that it is easier to choose a mount first and decide on a frame afterwards. This is because the mount will be placed next to the picture and so will have the bigger visual impact on it.

The frame must never overpower the picture. For example, a large, ornate frame will look totally out of place on a small water colour; the frame should match and complement the size and subtlety of the colour and form of the artwork. To help you make your decision, take the picture with you when you choose the frame or moulding; that way you can try a number of options until you find the right one.

Bear in mind that your choice of frame may also be determined by wider surroundings. If the picture is to be hung in a certain room, then the style, colour and general feel of that room should be considered. A framed picture should be worthy of note, but should not suffer the indignity of looking out of place. Choose a plain frame for a modern room and a textured frame for a more traditional room. Having said this, an ornate antique frame can look wonderful with modern decor but it

Mountboard comes in a huge range of colours; these (left) are just a few. Being right next to the picture, the colour of the mount has a strong visual impact, so it may be easier to select the mount first and choose a frame to complete the overall effect.

takes daring to carry it off. If the room has patterned wallpaper, then a plain frame will establish a boundary around the work.

Remember that art is a matter of personal taste. Creating a picture is an art and framing it is an art, so experiment until the combination of frame and picture gives the desired impression, both in terms of an individual piece of art, and its position when hung. Change the combination if it doesn't give the right effect - there is more than one correct way to frame each picture.

The vivid colours of these poppies (below left) would overwhelm a coloured frame. Therefore, a thin stained wood and gold frame has been chosen to create a neutral boundary around this impressive picture. Without the marbled strip, (below right) this picture could look lost in such a big frame. The border balances the picture, while the frame helps to maintain its Italian feel. This frame (bottom left) is part of the overall image, with the moss and pebbles adding to the seaside theme. The fine lines around this architectural print (bottom right) add substance to an otherwise small picture and the gold frame lends to the traditional feel.

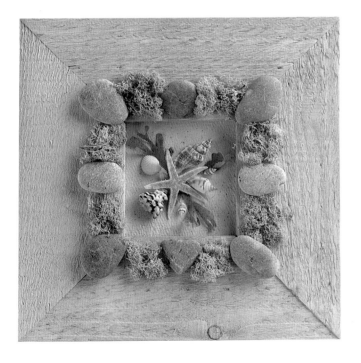

SELECTING A FRAME

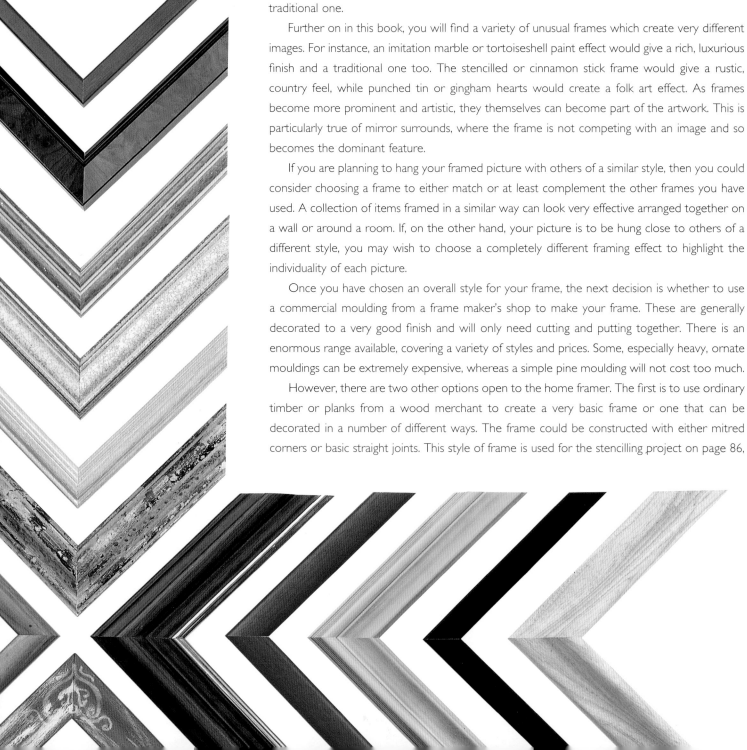

When deciding what type of frame or moulding to choose for your picture, the first aspect to consider is the general feel you wish to convey. Just the colour of the frame can have quite an effect on an image and will produce a substantial difference to the overall impression. If you choose a brightly-coloured frame that contrasts with the artwork you will create a contemporary feel, a polished oak or gilt frame will create a traditional one.

Further on in this book, you will find a variety of unusual frames which create very different images. For instance, an imitation marble or tortoiseshell paint effect would give a rich, luxurious finish and a traditional one too. The stencilled or cinnamon stick frame would give a rustic, country feel, while punched tin or gingham hearts would create a folk art effect. As frames become more prominent and artistic, they themselves can become part of the artwork. This is particularly true of mirror surrounds, where the frame is not competing with an image and so becomes the dominant feature.

If you are planning to hang your framed picture with others of a similar style, then you could consider choosing a frame to either match or at least complement the other frames you have used. A collection of items framed in a similar way can look very effective arranged together on a wall or around a room. If, on the other hand, your picture is to be hung close to others of a different style, you may wish to choose a completely different framing effect to highlight the individuality of each picture.

Once you have chosen an overall style for your frame, the next decision is whether to use a commercial moulding from a frame maker's shop to make your frame. These are generally decorated to a very good finish and will only need cutting and putting together. There is an enormous range available, covering a variety of styles and prices. Some, especially heavy, ornate mouldings can be extremely expensive, whereas a simple pine moulding will not cost too much.

However, there are two other options open to the home framer. The first is to use ordinary timber or planks from a wood merchant to create a very basic frame or one that can be decorated in a number of different ways. The frame could be constructed with either mitred corners or basic straight joints. This style of frame is used for the stencilling project on page 86,

Frames can be made in virtually any profile, colour or pattern; this is a selection (left) of plainer varieties suitable for a wide range of pictures. The tortoiseshell frame (above) was selected so that the warm tones of the tortoiseshell would accentuate the delicate tones in the painting. The wide, pale mount has been put between the two to allow the colours to come out in the picture, and prevent it being overwhelmed by the frame. The cinnamon stick frame, however, is very dominant and was created in conjunction with the leaf collage for an overall, natural effect. No glass has been put in the frame - it would look out of place.

although you could use planed timber for a neater, smoother finish. The second option is to select a moulding or beading from a builder's merchant or DIY store. These mouldings are normally used for skirting boards, window frames, dado rails and around doorways and come in a variety of styles and widths and a choice of hard- or softwood. Obviously the wider mouldings would make a very substantial frame that would have to be used with care, but the narrower types would make good frames and at a fraction of the cost of a specially-designed frame moulding. The major difference between actual frame moulding and one bought from a DIY shop is that the real thing will have

a rebate built into the back into which the other frame elements fit. You will have to add your own rebate to a basic timber frame. The easiest solution is to glue and screw or nail four narrow wooden batons to the back of the frame to enclose the central window, but set a little way in from it; there are further details of the procedure for adding a rebate on page 25.

You could add further interest to your frame by creating a secondary inner frame, usually referred to as a slip frame. This can be used to merely enhance the outer frame, but can also be a very useful device to add if the frame is too large for the artwork. You can create an inner frame to bridge the gap. A slip frame could be made from a complementary material such as gilt, or covered in a rich fabric such as velvet which lends itself well to oil paintings.

Remember that there is no one correct way to frame any particular picture and that the choice is really more a matter of taste. There are, however, a number of practical guidelines which should be taken into consideration, such as using a strong frame for a heavy oil, and protecting a water colour behind glass and a mount. These aspects are discussed on the next page.

PRACTICAL ASPECTS

Although there should be no limitations, other than personal taste, on the type of frame which is chosen for a picture, there are a few practicalities which must be considered depending on the type of work you are framing. A frame is not only used for its aesthetic qualities, but also for the protection it offers the picture. Different media require different framing treatments and here you will find a few general guidelines.

Oils and acrylics

Most oils and acrylics are painted onto canvas stretched taut over a wooden frame, although some are painted on wooden boards. Canvas can cause some difficulties as it may become distorted or puckered, and the folds in the corners can give it an irregular thickness. When choosing a frame, ensure the rebate is deep enough to accommodate the canvas and the frame strong enough to prevent it moving. Oils and acrylics give the framer a wide choice in framing styles. Even a small painting, if bold enough, can be framed in a wide moulding to give it much greater presence. The paints themselves are strong enough not to need protection from glass.

Water colours and pastels

Traditional water colours have a transparent, fragile quality and should be framed in a discreet way. Often a simple frame in wood or a pale colour will benefit the character of the painting. Glass is needed to protect the painted surface and also stop it getting dusty. A mount is used to hold the glass away from the surface of the picture, but can of course also be used as a visual tool. Pastels are even more vulnerable and should be protected in the same way. Often pastel colours are much bolder than water colours and the framing style should reflect this.

The Thai dancer (below left) is printed on fabric which has been stuck on top of mountboard, allowing the edges of the linen to be seen. Glass protects it from dust. Small oil paintings, like this still life, benefit from an elaborate frame, giving the picture greater size and impact. Water colours and photographs, like those below, need to be protected from wear so should always be framed with glass and a mount to hold the glass off the surface of the picture. Both have neutral frames which do not compete with the image, the composition in the case of the photograph and the strong colours in the case of the water colour.

Photographs

Photographic paper is not very hard wearing so you will need glass and a mount. Old photographs look best framed in a style from the same era, perhaps with two or more pictures in the same frame. Modern photographs need a modern approach. Black and whites, for example, benefit from a simple black or metallic frame which won't detract from the graphic image.

Three-dimensional objects

There will be instances when you want to frame objects such as shells or souvenirs for display, like the Indian beadwork on page 7. You will need a box frame, which is made in the same way as a normal frame, but with a much deeper moulding to create the space. Use glass in the frame to exclude dust.

Posters

Posters are designed to be temporary pieces of art, so it would seem inappropriate to treat them in a traditional, lasting way. An inexpensive clip frame or plain, narrow moulding would be best.

SELECTING A MOUNT

Choosing a mount to suit your picture can seem a rather daunting task given the huge array of mountboards and papers available today. There is not only the colour to consider, but also the surface texture - you will find mountboard in matt, shiny, linen effect and so on. There is also the option of creating your own textures and colours by sticking a sheet of paper over the mountboard - handmade papers can look very effective with their natural, soft surface. Whatever you choose, it is important to ensure the proportions are correct and this usually means making the mount wider at the bottom than on the other three sides to balance the overall effect.

There are no hard and fast rules as to the size of mount you should use so you will need to decide what you think best displays the picture. If you choose a wide mount for a small picture, it is probably preferable to choose a neutral colour such as grey, cream or a pastel shade, depending on the colours in the picture. When carefully selected, a wide mount can make a small picture appear more prominent and impressive; a small picture with a narrow mount can often seem insignificant, partly because the overall framed item will be smaller. Even if you intend to hang a group of small pictures together, you will often find that wider mounts will still add to the impact and show each picture to its best advantage.

When choosing a mount for larger subjects, it often helps to use the composition of the picture as a guide. If the style is loose with a fair amount of empty space, a narrow mount may be more suitable. Alternatively, try using a double mount with a narrow mount in a dark colour closest to the picture and a wide, paler mount around the outside. The inner mount will act as a distinct outline around the picture to help define its boundaries, but you will still have the width of the wider mount if you want it. If the picture is busy or comprises strong colours, make the mount any size you like, but bear in mind that it does create a relief between the picture and frame so a wider mount may be preferable. However, on large pictures, a wide mount could be impractical and make the overall size of the picture too large to be displayed easily on the wall.

The colour of the mount greatly affects how we see the picture. By picking out a colour from the picture, like the pink, yellow, blue and green mounts (left), that colour becomes more dominant. This is particularly obvious with the blue mount; it picks out the dark blue tones making the picture seem heavy and dark. The cream mount makes the picture seem brighter, but perhaps isn't strong enough to make a distinct boundary around it. The red mount is wholly unsuitable - the colour is far too dominant and is not in any way related to the picture. Mountboard tends to come in flat shades of colour (far left), but if you should want a soft, mottled effect, why not consider sticking handmade paper, like the cream, pink and green examples, onto the front of a plain mount? You can't use the paper alone as its depth would not be enough to hold the glass off the surface of the picture.

CHAPTER TWO

BASIC
TECHNIQUES

The skills needed for basic frame making are quite simple and won't take long to master. With the increasing popularity of picture framing at home, the necessary equipment is becoming more easily available. This section takes you, step by step, through the process of frame making from the initial measuring up to the final assembly of frame, glass, mount and backing board. With this basic knowledge, together with a little practice and confidence, you will soon be ready to take on more complicated projects. Always pay attention to accurate measurements and cutting to achieve a really professional finish.

HOW TO BEGIN

B efore embarking on a project, you will need to master the basic skills needed to make a frame. This is not as difficult as you may think - in fact, most of the skills needed are straightforward and can be mastered quickly. The frame is made up of five different elements. First there is the frame itself which is made from four lengths of moulding. Next is the glass which needs to fit snugly inside the frame, and behind the glass comes the mount which forms a border around the picture and holds the glass away from it. Then comes the picture and lastly the backing board, usually made from hardboard, which is pinned in place at the back of the frame to keep everything protected and secure. At all stages of frame making, the most important point is to make sure all measurements are correct. The glass, mount and backing board must fit perfectly in the rebate of the moulding and the window must be cut exactly square. Any discrepancies will show clearly when the frame is assembled.

You do not need expensive tools to make your own frames, and you may already have most of the tools needed. Probably the most important are a sharp tenon saw and mitre block for

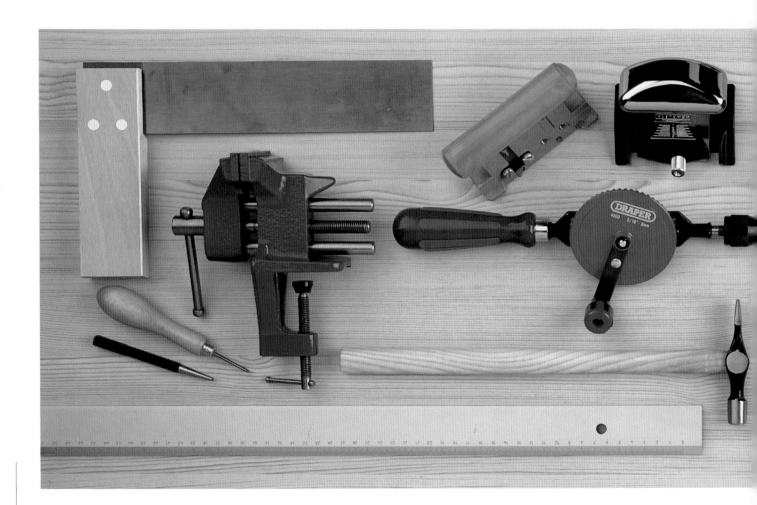

cutting the frame corners. If you intend to do a lot of frame making, it would be a good idea to invest in a proper mitre saw for more accurate cutting. You will also need a clamp to hold the frame square while it is being glued together; a strap clamp is inexpensive and effective. The other two pieces of specialist equipment are both easy to find: the first is a handheld mount cutter for cutting perfect bevelled edges and the other is a glass cutter which looks rather like a pen, but has a small steel wheel at the end. These can be purchased from craft or DIY suppliers.

A frame consists of five separate elements (right): the basic moulding, the glass behind, the mount, the picture itself, and a piece of hardboard at the back to hold everything in place. Some of the tools you may need to make a frame are (below, clockwise from top left) a tri-square for marking out perfect 90° angles, two mount cutters for cutting bevelled edges, hand drill for making pilot holes in hardwood frames, mitre cutting clamp, sharp knife for trimming moulding ends, electric drill, G-clamp, tenon saw, pliers, glass cutter, small hammer for panel pins, heavy rule, table vice, nail punch and bradawl for making pilot holes in softwood.

MAKING A BASIC FRAME

The method for making a basic frame is quite straightforward. The principles shown in this section will apply to all levels of frame making from the simple frame we make here to more complicated or ornate frames. Once you have acquired these basic skills, you will have a good base from which to work and as your experience grows, the better your technique will become and so you will have the confidence to embark on more demanding and satisfying projects which you could design yourself.

When starting out in home frame making, the most basic requirement is to have a good, solid, level surface to work on, albeit the kitchen table initially. Next, a small range of tools will be needed together with a decent straight edge or rule. The most important point to obtaining good results is to ensure the frame is perfectly square. You can force corners together or fill gaps with wood filler, but the final result is always disappointing. It also becomes increasingly difficult to fit the glass, mount and backing board into an off-square frame, apart from the fact that discrepancies will show clearly when you hang the frame on a wall. Double checking all your

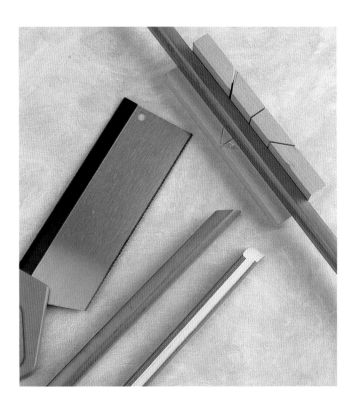

1. Using a mitre block and sharp tenon saw, cut the first angle carefully through the moulding, making sure it is lying flat on the block. Mark the position for the next corner on the outside edge of the moulding, turn the moulding around and cut another mitre. Repeat with all four sides.

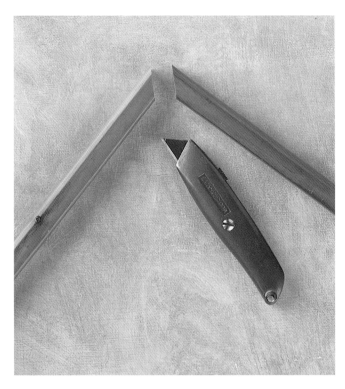

2. When all four sides are cut, place each pair of cut ends face to face to check they fit snugly together. If you find that they need to be trimmed for a more accurate fit, use a sharp knife to pare off the excess, leaving a flat, even surface. Do not use sandpaper or you may round off the ends, preventing a good fit.

measurements is crucial to ensure a good final result. If you start out making sure all measurements are accurate, you will save a lot of time trying to put things right later on.

To make a basic square or rectangular frame, the end of each piece of moulding has to be cut at 45°, with the outside edge of the moulding longer at both ends than the inside edge. The four pieces of moulding are joined together at the cut ends to form the corners, in what is called a mitre joint. It is important to ensure the opposite sides of the frame are of equal length, so exact measurement is essential.

You may find it easier to calculate the size of frame you need by cutting the mountboard first and using it as a guide to cutting the frame pieces. Take note of the external dimensions of the

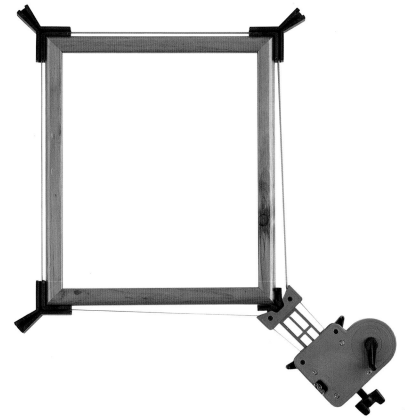

A strap clamp (right) is probably the best clamp to start with, being easy to use and inexpensive. The four plastic corners hold the frame together while the glue is drying. The corners are held in place with a fabric strap which can be tightened with the screw to fit your frame and hold the sides firmly in place.

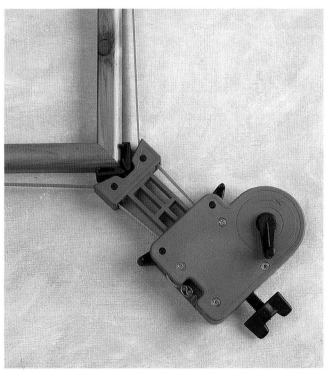

3. Brush any saw dust or parings off the cut ends, then apply glue and press the joints together. Repeat with all four corners to make the basic frame shape. Use PVA or wood glue, depending on the thickness of the moulding. A heavy frame will really need a strong wood glue to hold it together before it is nailed.

4. The frame will need to be held square with a specially-designed clamp while the glue dries. Fit the clamp around the frame, following the manufacturer's instructions as to how to tighten it. Leave on a flat surface until the glue is thoroughly dry - overnight to be sure.

mount and the width of the moulding to be used to make the frame (minus the width of the rebate which will overlap the mount). To calculate the external dimensions of the frame needed, add the length (or width) of the mountboard to twice the width of the moulding, adding a little bit extra for a more comfortable fit.

Once all the sizes have been calculated, you can start to cut the moulding to fit. Cut one end of the first piece of moulding using a sharp tenon saw with either a mitre block or a mitre clamp to make the 45° angle. You could use a specially-designed mitre saw for a more accurate cut. Make sure you are cutting on a flat surface; if the moulding or clamp tilts, your angle will not be accurate. Mark the correct length on the outside edge of the moulding and cut another mitre, this time facing in the opposite direction. When the first piece is cut at both ends, use it as a pattern for the opposite side of the frame, measuring each length carefully. Remember to make sure that the outer edge of each piece of moulding is longer at both ends than the inner

edge. Repeat the process with the other two sides, always making sure you are cutting the mitre the right way round. If the frame is square, you could use the first side as a template for the other three sides.

Trim any rough edges with a knife or chisel if the joints do not fit snugly together, paring off a little at a time and all the while keeping the bare edge flat and smooth. Don't be tempted to use sandpaper on the cut mitres as you may round the edges and prevent the joints fitting together properly. Use PVA or wood glue on the joints and press them firmly together. To hold the frame in position while the glue is drying, you will need a specially-designed clamp. There are lots on the market, but the easiest is probably a strap clamp which consists of four corners and a strap which exerts pressure around the frame as it is tightened.

Remove the clamp when the glue is dry and the frame is rigid. Hammer a small panel pin through each frame corner to strengthen it. A small frame like the one we have made will only

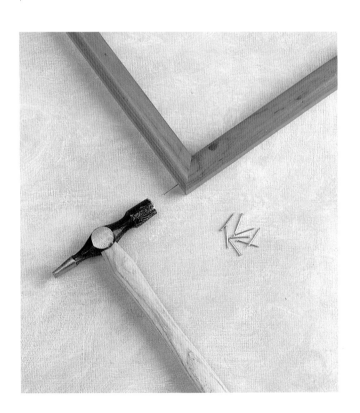

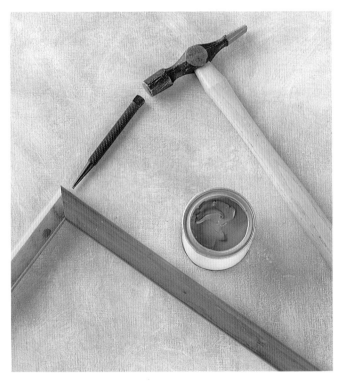

5. Remove the frame from the clamp and strengthen the corners with panel pins, one through each corner. On a softwood frame, make shallow pilot holes for the pins using a bradawl and hammer the pins in place. On hardwood, drill deep holes to prevent damage to the frame through the heavier hammering required.

6. When the pins are almost in, use a nail punch to finish off. This will prevent you from damaging the frame with the hammer. Drive the pins in until the heads are just below the surface of the wood. Fill the pin holes with a wood filler to match the colour of your wood. When dry, sand the filler smooth.

need one pin per side, but larger frames will need more. If the frame is made from hardwood, you will need to drill quite deep pilot holes in which to hammer the nails as heavy hammering may cause the frame to fall apart. Whether you use a hand or electric drill, be sure to choose the right drill bit as the size is quite important. A bradawl will be sufficient to make pilot holes on softwood frames. When the nails have been hammered in most of the way, finish them off with a nail punch, driving the head just below the surface of the wood. This will protect the frame from being dented by the hammer. Fill the holes above the nail heads with a wood filler to match the colour of the frame. When dry, smooth the surface with fine sandpaper, taking care not to remove any finish on the frame.

Creating a rebate

Many of the projects you will find in this book end up as basic two-dimensional frames, so you will need to create a rebate on the back into which the glass, mount and backing board fit and are held in position.

The simplest method is to glue and screw four wooden batons to the back, set in from the inner edges of the frame. The glass, mount and backing board are cut larger than the inner window of the frame to fit just inside the batons. The batons can be any width, so long as they do not protrude beyond the outer edges of the frame and they leave enough of a margin along the inner edges. Make sure the batons are not too deep, or they will hold the frame away from the wall when you hang the picture.

The rebate can be added before or after you decorate the frame. If you are covering a frame with fabric, for example, it would be better to add the rebate after you do this.

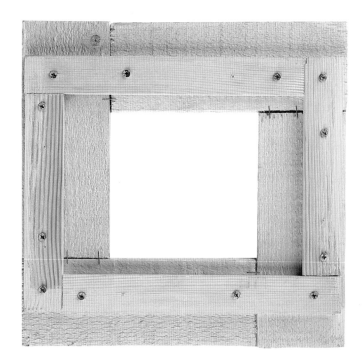

A basic flat frame will need to have a rebate added to the back, to hold the glass, mount and backing board in position. This frame (right) has the most basic type of rebate: four thin batons of wood arranged on the back of the frame a little way in from the inside edges. The batons are screwed or nailed in position and the glass, mount and backing board are cut so they fit snugly up against the batons on all four sides. As an alternative to traditional mitred corners, the frame above right has been made using four planks of recycled pallet wood with square ends. The planks are cut to equal lengths and then glued together into a square. Staples are added along each joint for extra strength. This type of frame is very simple to make and lends itself well to a rustic feel, like the stencilled frame on page 86. To make a rectangular frame, cut two short planks and two long planks and arrange in the same way.

CUTTING A MOUNT

Before you start cutting a mount, you need to consider how wide you want it to be. This will depend on the effect you are trying to create. You will also need to bear in mind that it is general practice to make the mount wider at the bottom of the picture than at the top or the sides. This is because if you cut all the sides to the same width, the bottom margin always looks narrower than the others; this is just an optical illusion.

Cutting the inner window is not at all difficult if you are happy with a vertical edge; all you need is a sharp knife and ruler. However, the majority of mounts are cut with a bevelled edge and this is achieved by the use of a mount cutter. There are a number of different ones available which will cut smoothly through the mountboard at an angle of 45°. The most difficult part of the process is cutting the corners neatly, but if you read the manufacturer's guidelines and practise a little first, you should be able to achieve a satisfactory finish.

Before you start to cut the mount, lay the picture on the mountboard to calculate the size you would like. Then cut it out with a sharp knife and ruler. Mark the position of the window on

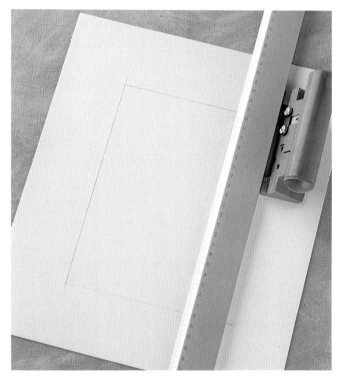

1. Cut the mountboard to the size required using a sharp craft knife and metal ruler. Turn the mountboard over and mark the position of the inner window on the back, referring to the picture you are framing as a guide. Remember to make the bottom margin wider than those at the top and sides.

2. Make sure all measurements are correct before you cut the mount. Lay the ruler along the pencil line and run the mount cutter along it two or three times until the mountboard is cut through. Remember to extend each cut by the thickness of the mountboard at both ends. Repeat with the other three sides.

the back of the mount, again using the picture as a guide. Check to see whether your mount cutter cuts the board a certain distance from the ruler and if it does, alter your measurements accordingly.

Lay the ruler on the mount and slowly run the cutter along it. You will need to extend each cut by the thickness of the mountboard at either end to make sure the corners meet. You may need to run the cutter along the ruler two or three times before it cuts through. Work your way clockwise around the window until it is complete. Before removing the central square, make sure it is cut through right the way round, or you may tear it. Any rough edges can be carefully smoothed down with a fine grade sandpaper or trimmed with a sharp knife.

As an alternative, you could make a double mount (top right), a double thickness mount (centre), or triple mount (bottom right). Double and triple mounts make use of two or three mounts of different colours cut to different sizes, whereas a double thickness mount uses two thickness of mountboard cut together.

3. Check the mount is cut right through before removing the window, otherwise you may tear the mountboard, leaving an untidy edge. Any rough or uneven sections on the bevelled edge can be lightly sanded with a fine grade sandpaper or trimmed with a sharp knife.

CUTTING GLASS

Glass cutting is generally considered as something not to be attempted at home, but it is not as difficult as you may think as long as you follow the basic procedure and, of course, take care - wear thick gloves if you are worried. Most glass suppliers will cut a piece to the size you require, and if you need a very large pane of glass, it is probably better to get a professional to cut it for you. But if you should need to cut an existing pane down to size, here's how to do it safely.

First find a flat, stable surface on which to place the glass. You will also need a glass cutting tool. There are various different types available, but the easiest for beginners to use is a handheld cutter, about the size of a pen, with a revolving steel wheel. Lay the glass flat and mark on it the size you require using a fibre tipped pen and ruler.

Before you start, lubricate the cutter with white spirit or oil. Lay a ruler along the line you have marked. You may prefer to use a rubber-backed ruler which will not slip while you are cutting. Hold the ruler in place with one hand and roll the cutter along the ruler with the other.

1. Measure the space at the back of your frame which is bordered by the rebate. This will be slightly larger than the size of the frame window. Mark out the size on the piece of glass using a fibre tipped pen and ruler. Check all the measurements again, then check the corners are square.

2. Lay the glass on a smooth surface. Lubricate the glass cutter to make the wheel turn more freely. Lay a ruler along the marked line and score along it once with the glass cutter, maintaining even pressure. The amount of pressure needed will come with practice, so try out the technique on scrap glass first.

Do this only once. The intention is to exert pressure on the glass to achieve an even score line, not to actually cut through it.

The next step is to break the glass along the score line. Most cutters have a round knob on the end of the handle with which to tap along the score until the glass breaks. Another method is to hold the glass with one hand on either side of the score line and literally snap it in two by exerting even pressure on both sides. The last, probably safer, way is to lay the glass on top of a ruler on a table, with the edge of the ruler along the score line. Press down firmly on both sides of the ruler and the glass should break neatly along the edge. If you find the glass does not break exactly along the whole length of the score line, trim off the extra pieces using glass breaking pliers.

Handheld glass cutters are simple tools to use. These two, right, are good examples. All consist of a revolving steel wheel at one end with which to score the glass and a round knob at the other to tap the glass and break it along the score line. Pliers are used to snip off pieces of glass which are too small to handle.

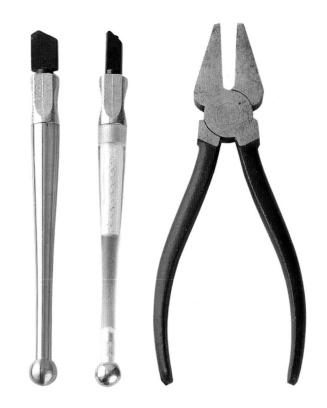

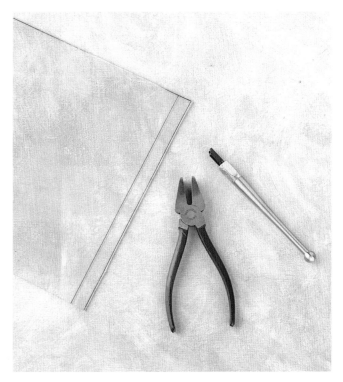

3. If you have a glass cutter with a heavy knob at the end, use this to tap the glass along the score line, while the glass is still lying flat. The glass should break neatly in two. If you do not have a cutter with a knob, lay the score line along the edge of a ruler on the work surface and press both sides until the glass breaks.

4. If the glass has not broken smoothly along the whole length of the score line, or if you need to remove just a small strip of glass, use special glass breaking pliers to snip off the pieces. Work your way along the line, trimming off small pieces at a time until the edge is smooth.

ASSEMBLING THE FRAME

Now all the parts of the frame are ready, there is one last thing to do before assembling them, and that is to cut a backing board. This is usually made from hardboard which should be cut to the same size as the piece of glass and the mount. Hardboard can be scored with a sharp knife and then snapped along the score line to leave a neat edge. Thick hardboard will need to be cut to size with a saw.

To assemble the frame elements, lay the frame itself face down on a work surface. Clean the glass on both sides to make sure it is free from grease and dust, then lay it in the frame, inside the rebate. Seal the glass in place using gumstrip, available from picture frame or artist's supply shops. Stick a length of gumstrip along each edge of the back of the glass and fold the excess up the inside edges of the frame rebate. This will stop dust getting in the front of the frame. Next attach the picture to the back of the mount using gumstrip or acid-free tape, taking care to align the image centrally in the mount window. Lay the mount and picture face down on the glass in the frame, then place the backing board on top to hold everything tightly in position.

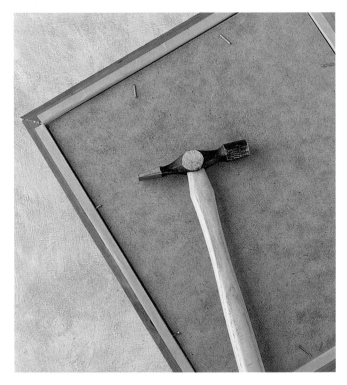

1. Make sure the glass is clean before fitting it into the frame. Seal it into the frame with gumstrip to prevent dust coming in the front of the frame. Stick the gumstrip along the edges of the glass and stick the excess up the inner edges of the frame. Take care not to let the gumstrip show at the front of the frame.

2. Stick the picture on the back of the mount, positioning the image centrally in the mount window. Place face down in the frame, and lay the backing board on top. Hammer small pins into the inside edges of the frame to hold the backing board in place. You could use a nail punch to prevent damage to the frame.

Before you pin the backing board into place, turn over the frame to check the picture is in the right position and there is no dust or dirt behind the glass. When you are satisfied, turn the frame back over and hammer in small pins to hold the backing board in place. Space the pins evenly around the frame and tap into the sides of the frame at an angle, trapping the edges of the board underneath. Stick a length of gumstrip down all four sides of the frame to cover the gap alongside the edge of the backing board and seal it in place.

Finally add the appropriate hangings. If you want the frame to lay flat against the wall, use fastening plates, otherwise screw eyelets into the back of the frame and thread picture wire or nylon cord between them.

There are numerous wall fixings and hangings available, and these (right) are a small selection. Hanging plates like the two top right and the one bottom left are strong enough to support heavy frames. Lighter frames can be supported with eyelets threaded with picture wire, hung from picture hooks or pins in the wall.

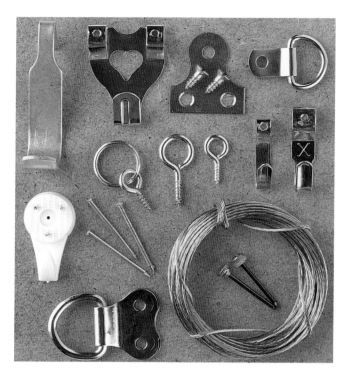

3. You will need to seal everything in place to stop dust getting in to the frame and showing inside the glass. Use gumstrip, wetting it thoroughly with a damp sponge, to cover the gap down all four sides between the backing board and the frame. Allow the gumstrip to dry thoroughly.

4. Eyelets threaded with picture wire will be suitable hangings for most frames. Use a bradawl to make a hole in each side of the frame, about one quarter of the way down from the top. Screw an eyelet into each hole and thread nylon cord or picture wire between them, as tightly as possible.

CHAPTER THREE

PAINT
FINISHES

Due to the renewed popularity of paint finishes, there is now a wide range of commercial paint-finished frames available. However, many finishes should really be applied after the frame has been constructed to cover the mitred corners, so it is often better to do them yourself. Many manufacturers have recognised the increased popularity and have developed new products and colours, such as ready made glazes and stains, and even slow-drying emulsion. Applying a paint finish can give you great satisfaction, but it must be approached with confidence; so relax and experiment a little first.

MARBLING

Marbling is a classic technique resulting in a subtle, softly mottled effect in rich tones. It does take a little bit of practice to get a perfect finish, but it is not impossible, as long as you bear in mind two points. First, choose a relatively flat frame to work on. If the frame has lots of ridges and crevices, it will be very difficult to achieve a good finish.

Secondly, more can be less. In other words, when painting imitation marble, you are not trying to achieve an exact replica of the real thing. You are trying to create a pleasing finish based on the subtleties of marble. Therefore you may find that once you have created a good, ragged base colour, it will only need the minimum of additional finish to complete it.

If you feel that a marble finish on the whole frame may be a little too overpowering, you may consider painting just the inner section and leaving the outer portion in a plain colour. Obviously you would have to choose the frame carefully to ensure the shape of the moulding lends itself to this type of treatment.

1. Paint the frame with off-white eggshell. Mix a glaze using two parts white spirit to one of linseed oil. Mix raw sienna oil paint into some of the glaze and apply to the frame in thin washes. Repeat with a grey violet glaze, this time ragging it on.

2. When you have built up irregular patches of colour, soften the effect by gently patting a soft brush over the frame. Before the glaze dries, moisten a small sponge with white spirit and use to spatter the surface. Soften again with the brush.

3. While the glaze is still wet, cut a small square of cotton rag and use the very edge to drag across the surface of the frame, cutting through the glaze. The rag will leave fine white lines to suggest white veins. Soften the effect with the brush.

4. Make another glaze using raw sienna, grey violet and black oil paints. Use a fine artist's brush to paint on fine lines to resemble the dark veins in natural marble. Again, soften the lines with a brush and leave to dry. Varnish the frame to protect.

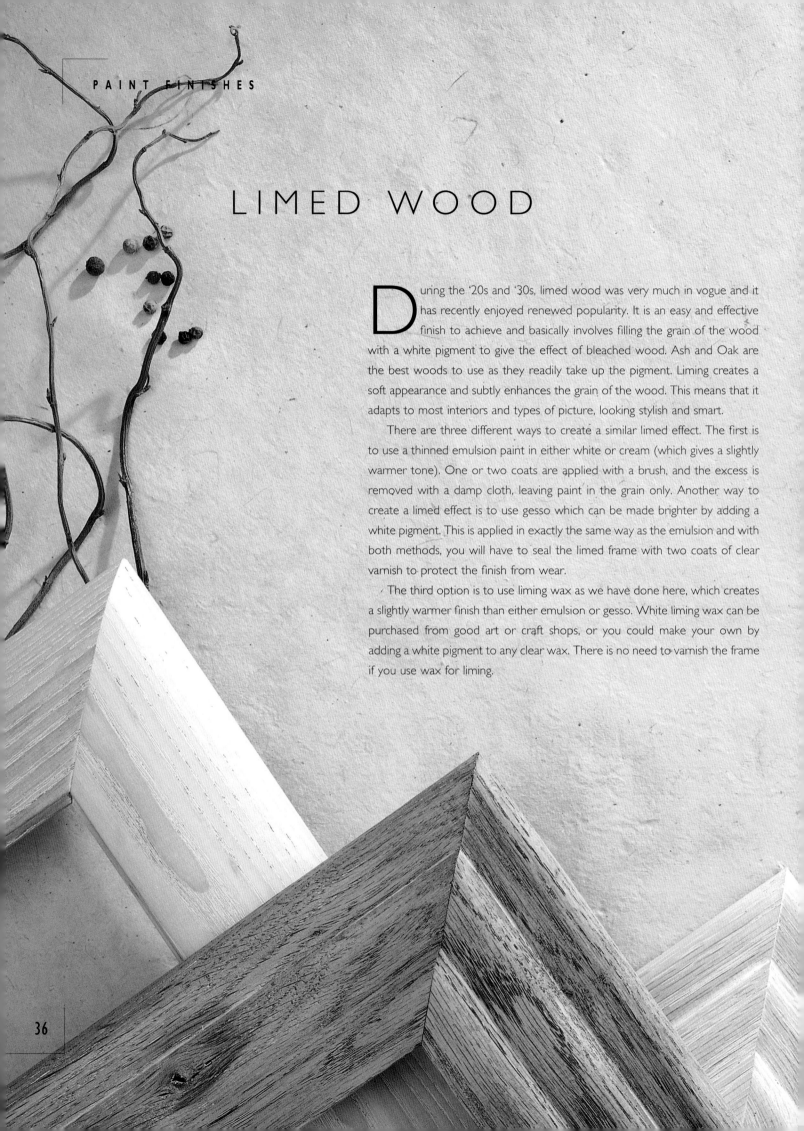

LIMED WOOD

During the '20s and '30s, limed wood was very much in vogue and it has recently enjoyed renewed popularity. It is an easy and effective finish to achieve and basically involves filling the grain of the wood with a white pigment to give the effect of bleached wood. Ash and Oak are the best woods to use as they readily take up the pigment. Liming creates a soft appearance and subtly enhances the grain of the wood. This means that it adapts to most interiors and types of picture, looking stylish and smart.

There are three different ways to create a similar limed effect. The first is to use a thinned emulsion paint in either white or cream (which gives a slightly warmer tone). One or two coats are applied with a brush, and the excess is removed with a damp cloth, leaving paint in the grain only. Another way to create a limed effect is to use gesso which can be made brighter by adding a white pigment. This is applied in exactly the same way as the emulsion and with both methods, you will have to seal the limed frame with two coats of clear varnish to protect the finish from wear.

The third option is to use liming wax as we have done here, which creates a slightly warmer finish than either emulsion or gesso. White liming wax can be purchased from good art or craft shops, or you could make your own by adding a white pigment to any clear wax. There is no need to varnish the frame if you use wax for liming.

1. Make sure the frame is free from dirt and grease before you begin. Remove greasy fingerprints or stains using a soft cloth and white spirit. Any stubborn marks can be removed by rubbing lightly with fine grade glass paper.

2. Use a fine grade steel wool to apply the liming wax freely to the wood, working it well into the grain and into crevices in the moulding. Make sure you treat the inner frame edge in the same way as it will be visible when the frame is in use.

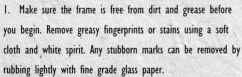

3. Take off the excess wax using a soft cloth and white spirit or turpentine. You can remove practically all of it to give a subtle limed effect, or only a little to create a lighter, more bleached appearance.

4. An optional last stage is to apply a black wax on top to deepen the colour and give a rich tone. Apply the wax using fine steel wool and continue to rub the frame until the wax starts to come off again, leaving a thin sheen.

TORTOISESHELL

The warm, mellow tone of tortoiseshell lends itself well to a frame. It is a somewhat unusual and rather exotic finish, but used carefully and not overdone, it makes a very interesting frame. Because of the strong, bold nature of the pattern, it will be most effective on a very simple frame without recesses in the moulding.

It is quite easy to achieve a fairly good replica of natural tortoiseshell, especially if you apply enough high gloss varnish to give the frame a really deep sheen. But do remember that it is a paint finish and not the real thing, and you can therefore change the tones to suit the picture you are going to frame or the room in which you intend to hang it.

You can create a dark tortoiseshell as we have here using a yellow base coat and applying spots of raw sienna, burnt sienna and raw umber oil paints to make the pattern. Alternatively, if you want a much lighter effect, apply a silver or pale yellow base coat and choose faun or lighter brown paints for the pattern, again choosing three different tones. This is often referred to as blond tortoiseshell. It is, of course, easy to create any number of different tones and effects by varying the base colour and the colours of your oil paints, so why not experiment?

1. Paint the frame with yellow eggshell and allow to dry. Apply a coat of thinned clear glaze over the top. Dab spots of raw sienna oil paint onto the wet glaze using a fine brush, then repeat with smaller and fewer spots of the darker burnt sienna.

2. As you are applying the paints, try to align the spots of colour in one direction to create a stripy appearance more like natural tortoiseshell. Finish off with spots of burnt umber over the other two colours.

3. Use a clean, soft brush to blend the colours together before they dry. Brush each part of the frame in one direction only to maintain the stripy pattern. Continue to blend the colours until you are satisfied with the result.

4. When the paint has dried, apply two coats of varnish, allowing the first coat to dry thoroughly before applying the second. It is important to choose a high gloss varnish to give the frame a deep sheen.

ANTIQUE GILT FINISH

The rich, sumptuous colour of this Baroque-style frame is achieved by applying layers of red gesso to a wooden frame and then buffing the final coat with gilt cream. Gesso is a traditional base often used in gilding and can be bought from most arts and crafts shops, where you will also find the gilt cream. Gesso consists of a fine mineral powder suspended in a medium which is often tinted with pigment like the one we have used here. We chose a dull red gesso to make a really rich base for the gold and bring an almost eastern feel to the frame.

The gesso is painted on to the frame in two or three coats, each one applied before the previous one has dried to create a strong skin. Once the gesso has thoroughly dried it can be sanded lightly to remove any lumps and bumps and give a smooth finish.

If you are unable to purchase gesso, similar results can be achieved using a matt oiled-based paint as a base. In this case, it is important to prime and undercoat the wood beforehand.

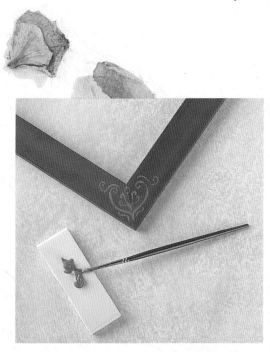

1. Melt the red gesso in a 'bain marie', following the manufacturer's instructions. Paint an even coat of gesso onto the frame facade using a paint brush. Just before the gesso is dry, apply a second coat.

2. When the base is completely dry, sand lightly to give a smooth finish. Paint a pattern in each corner of the frame using a fine paint brush and gold acrylic paint. Design your pattern on scrap paper beforehand to ensure the best results.

3. When the acrylic paint is dry, lightly re-paint over the pattern using gilt cream. Gently smudge the cream with a soft cloth to soften the lines of the design, giving it a distressed, antique appearance.

4. Rub a thin layer of gilt cream over the entire frame using your finger. You will only need to use a small amount of the cream as a little goes a long way. Buff the frame with a soft cloth to burnish the gold onto the base.

TARNISHED COPPER

Having included a number of more traditional paint finishes in this section, I thought it would be interesting to create a finish which would lend itself to a piece of modern or abstract art. This paint finish was designed to resemble tarnished copper; obviously it is not an exact replica, more a visual association.

The effect is achieved by building up layers of colour, starting with a green base coat. Patches of pine green and black are applied to emulate the verdigris tones of tarnished copper. Lastly, copper acrylic paint is added, both with a brush and spattered onto the frame to create spots of colour.

However, it would be just as effective to use this method with other colours. For instance, why not start with a base coat of turquoise rather than green, and add blue and gold to finish? This would look very good in a bathroom, perhaps framing a mirror. As with all paint finishes, try out different combinations of colour before you begin. It is often interesting to see the varied effects that can be achieved.

1. Apply a mid-green base coat and allow to dry. Mix pine green gouache with a little water and paint small areas of colour on the frame. Smear the paint with a bunched up rag, dabbing the curved areas and wiping it along the straight edges.

2. Thin black gouache in the same way and repeat the process, making sure you leave areas of green gouache and the base coat showing through. Next load some black gouache onto a brush and spatter it over the frame as described on page 46.

3. Thin some copper gouache and spatter this on top, then apply more to the frame using a fine artist's brush. Paint irregular patches into the crevices and onto the flat areas, constantly softening the edges with a clean rag as you go.

4. When the layers of gouache are completely dry, give the frame one or two coats of varnish, leaving the first to dry before applying the second. The varnish will not only protect the paint finish, but will also give the colours extra depth.

RAGGING

Ragging or rag rolling is a paint effect which has enjoyed renewed popularity in recent years. Used to give a soft, textured finish to painted wood and plain walls, it also lends itself well to decorating frames and is one of the easiest paint techniques to master.

The characteristic mottled finish is created by lifting off some of the surface colour while the paint is still wet. Rags, sponges, crumpled paper and even plastic can be used to create effective results and you might like to experiment beforehand on a spare piece of frame.

With this technique it is important to use a paint which doesn't dry too quickly. Oil-based paint can be mixed with a glaze bought from a paint supply shop or water-based paint can be mixed with wallpaper size to keep the paint wet for longer. The added medium delays the drying process and allows you sufficient time to achieve the desired effect.

Be careful when discarding the rag after you have finished. Oil-soaked rags are a fire hazard and should be left outdoors to dry naturally or disposed of safely.

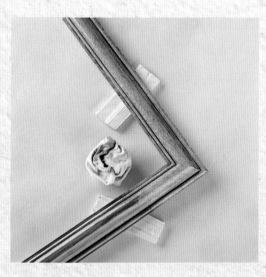

1. Paint the frame with primer and then with a coat of off-white eggshell. Mix equal amounts of glaze medium and white spirit to make a glaze base and then add enough artist's colour to achieve the required hue. Paint the glaze onto the frame.

2. Dab the glaze with a soft cloth to lift off the surface colour. As the cloth becomes soaked, re-fold and continue with a clean area. Pools of glaze in the grooves can be lifted using a small stippling brush to achieve a more even finish.

3. When the first glaze has dried, mix a second using a colour to complement the first. Apply in the same way, lifting off the excess colour with a soft cloth. The first glaze will show through the second giving depth and texture to the finished effect.

SPATTERED GRANITE

Spattering a frame with runny paint produces an effect reminiscent of natural granite, especially if you build up the finish with a number of different colours. This is probably the simplest paint effect to achieve and is great fun to do. You don't, of course, need to stick to natural granite colours; you could choose any combination of colours, but it will look most effective if those you choose are all quite similar to one another. You could pick three different shades of red, for example, or three reds and a dark grey to add a deeper tone to the frame.

The effect is achieved by holding a paint loaded brush over the frame and tapping the handle sharply on a firm object such as a ruler or the handle of a wooden spoon. Another method is to dip an old toothbrush in paint and to draw your fingers over the bristles, thereby flicking paint over the frame. The size of the drops you create will depend on how thick or thin the paint is. It is a good idea to experiment before you begin on the frame. A flat frame is the best choice; frames with curved profiles and recesses will not take on the drops evenly.

Remember that this is a very messy technique, so cover a large area with old newspapers to protect your work surface and wear protective clothing while spattering.

1. Paint the frame with off-white eggshell and allow to dry. Thin pale grey emulsion until runny, load a brush with the paint, then tap the handle of the brush on the handle of a wooden spoon over the frame, spattering it with drops of paint.

2. Work your way around the frame, reloading the brush as necessary. Do not put too much paint on the brush or the drops will be very large. When the pale grey paint has dried, repeat the process using a darker grey paint.

3. Finally spatter the frame with a third colour, this time a charcoal grey, in the same way. Also paint the inside and outside edges of the frame using this colour. When the paint is dry, apply a coat of satin finish varnish to seal and protect.

CHAPTER FOUR

FANTASTIC
FRAMES

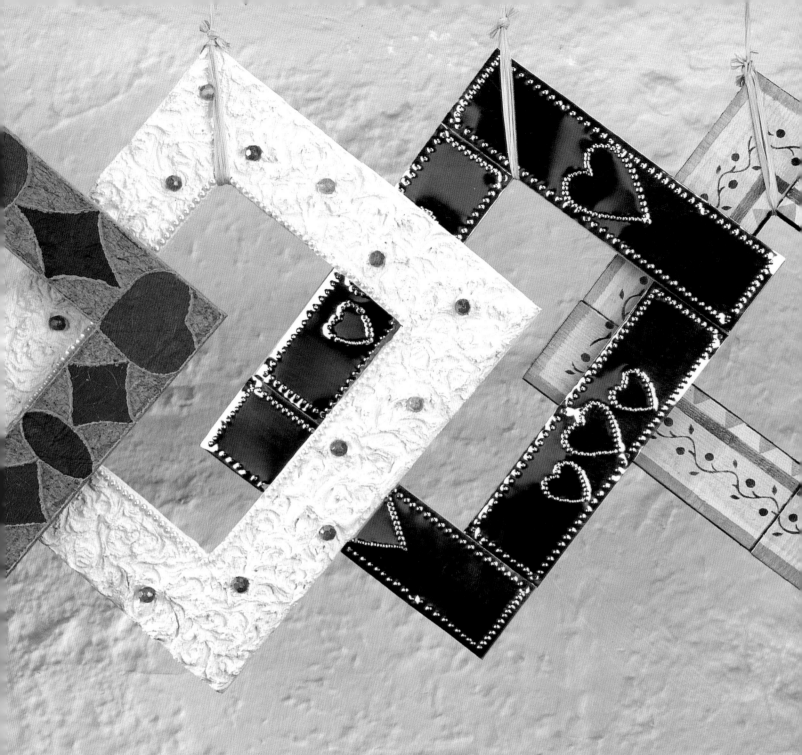

One of the fundamental rules in picture framing is that a frame is merely a border around a picture which should complement and never detract from it. However, you will find many frames in this section which challenge this traditional view. As tastes become more eclectic, then the frame can develop into a work of art itself and this is especially true when used on a mirror where it is not competing with an image. There are lots of ideas in this chapter using all kinds of materials. All of these projects will inspire you to create ideas to suit your own taste and, at the same time, challenge the traditional view.

SMART SPICE FRAME

Cinnamon has always been available as a culinary spice, but it can now be purchased from craft suppliers in a coated form. The coating makes the sticks harder, preventing them from crumbling when they are cut. This makes them far more suitable as a craft material. Also, the sticks available in craft shops tend to be longer than those bought for cooking. The basic cinnamon stick frame could be used as a base for other embellishments. You could add bundles of cinnamon sticks tied with tartan ribbon, or tied with corn ears and raffia for a country look. If you are framing a botanical collage, like the one on page 13, you could swap the bay leaves for ones similar to those in the picture, making the frame part of the total image.

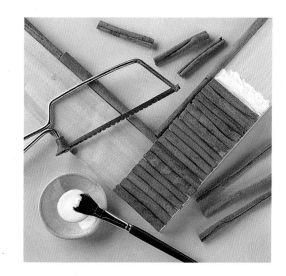

1. Select a number of long, straight cinnamon sticks to line the inside edge of the frame. This will create a slightly raised edge against which to butt the other sticks. Cut them to the right length with a hacksaw and glue in place.

2. Cut the remaining cinnamon sticks to the same width as the frame and glue to the frame in neat rows, butting them closely together. Arrange them vertically along the top and bottom edges and horizontally down the frame sides.

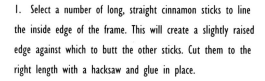

3. Choose six bay leaves of a similar size, shape and colour and glue them onto the frame, three down each side. Arrange the bay leaves so that they are equally spaced, with all the stalk ends pointing in the same direction.

4. If the outside edge of the wooden frame is bare wood or an unsuitable colour, stain it to match the cinnamon sticks using a wood stain. The same applies to any parts of the frame showing through the lines of cinnamon sticks.

WILLOW RING

Although this project was designed as a picture frame, it could also be used as a wall wreath, especially in a country kitchen. The frame starts off as a florist's wire wreath base, around which is twisted a series of fine willow wands to hide the wire. The wands are the fine, pliable stems from a Weeping Willow·tree; the leaves are stripped off and the woody parts are discarded to leave just the soft green stems.

Once you have made the basic willow frame, you can use your imagination to decorate it. We decorated one frame with dried oak leaves and acorn cups, but you could use small cones and twigs, dried hops, wheat ears or teasels instead. We decorated a second frame with dried apple and orange slices for a bolder, more unusual look. You can buy ready-dried fruit slices from craft suppliers, but it is simple to dry your own at home, and of course less expensive. Either slice the fruit thinly, arrange on a wire cooling rack and leave to dry in a warm, dark place; or place on absorbent paper on a non-metallic plate and microwave on a low setting in short bursts until the slices are dry.

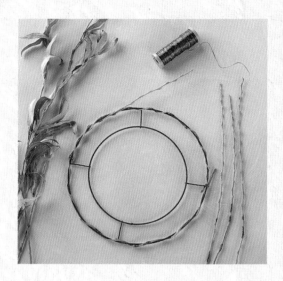

1. Wire the end of a willow wand to the outer ring of a wire wreath base and wind round and round the outer ring to cover the wire. Continue until the outer ring is covered, using as many pieces of willow as necessary and tucking in the ends.

2. Repeat to cover the inner ring. Then take a long piece of willow and wind around both rings together to create a zigzag pattern between them. Continue right around the ring, attaching the willow ends with reel wire.

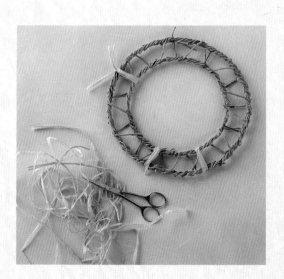

3. Next, choose some even pieces of natural raffia and wind round and round the wreath at intervals to create bunches to cover any wires that are showing. Knot the raffia strands on the outer edge of the ring to secure.

4. Glue your decorations around the frame, sticking them onto the raffia or willow wands using strong glue. Here we have chosen distinctively-shaped dried oak leaves and a few empty acorn cups to continue the theme and add more texture.

53

FOREST FRAME

Next time you decide to take a walk in the woods, don't forget to take a bag with you. It is quite amazing what you can find lying on the forest floor - cones, nuts, seedpods, dried leaves, bark and interesting twigs are just a few of the things. You can make a frame like this with practically anything and it can easily be adapted to include the items you have collected. The bark, twigs and cones are held onto the frame with tile adhesive which is more successful than basic glue when sticking randomly-shaped objects to a flat surface.

Do make sure, though, the tile adhesive is well covered with either dried leaves or bark pieces to give a good foundation for your design. Bark tends to grow in layers and the pieces you find on the forest floor will probably be dry. Therefore it should be easy to separate the layers into even flakes which will be easier to use on a frame than thick chunks.

When you are collecting material, remember that picking certain plants is against the law, so try to restrict yourself to those things you find on the ground, rather than taking them from living trees and other plants.

1. Start with a flat wood frame made by stapling together four lengths of sawn timber. Cover one of the outer edges of the frame with clear glue and stick a line of bark flakes on it to cover the wood. Leave to dry and repeat with the other edges.

2. Spread a thick layer of tile adhesive on the top third of the frame. Take long twigs and stick them into the adhesive with their loose ends pointing up to create a shaped top to the frame. Cover the bare adhesive with large curls of bark.

3. Spread tile adhesive over the rest of the frame and cover with more bark, cones, nuts and small twigs. Push the pieces into the adhesive to secure or glue where necessary, grouping the nuts and cones together for a natural look. Leave to dry.

4. Finish the frame by sticking dried leaves over any patches of visible tile adhesive, using a clear glue and a fine brush. You could, perhaps, choose yellow or red leaves to lift the brown tones of the other forest materials.

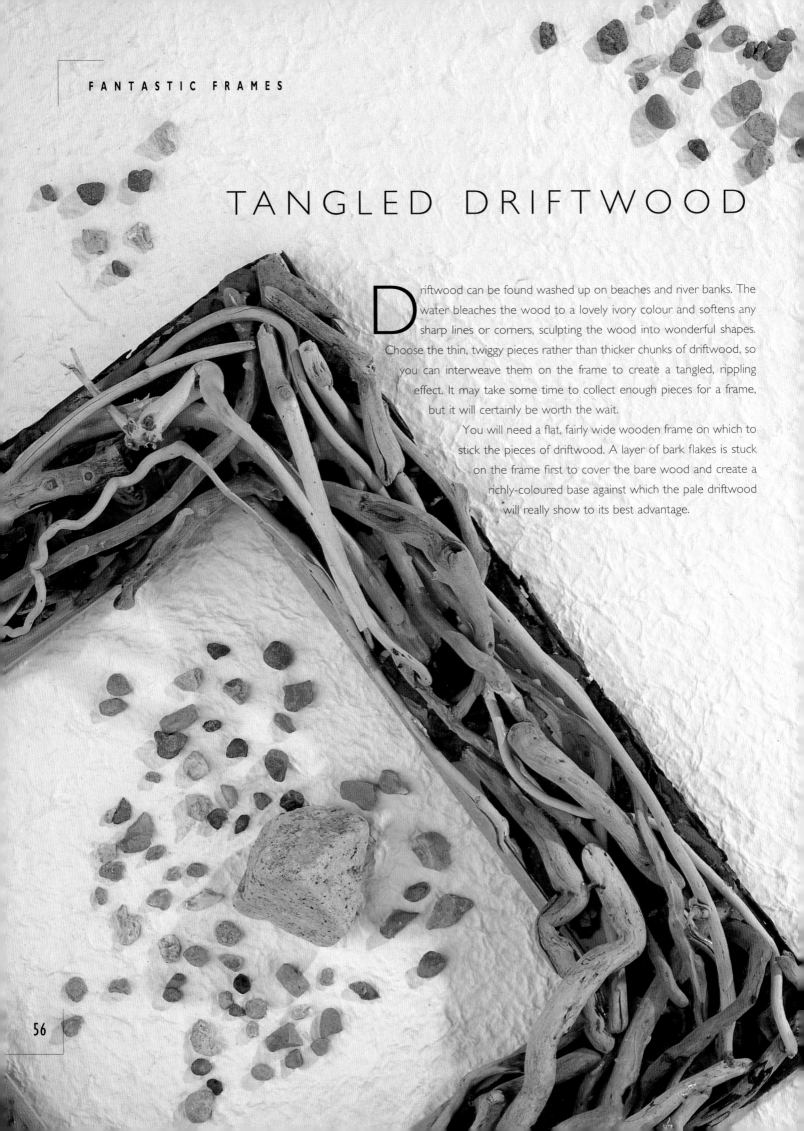

TANGLED DRIFTWOOD

Driftwood can be found washed up on beaches and river banks. The water bleaches the wood to a lovely ivory colour and softens any sharp lines or corners, sculpting the wood into wonderful shapes. Choose the thin, twiggy pieces rather than thicker chunks of driftwood, so you can interweave them on the frame to create a tangled, rippling effect. It may take some time to collect enough pieces for a frame, but it will certainly be worth the wait.

You will need a flat, fairly wide wooden frame on which to stick the pieces of driftwood. A layer of bark flakes is stuck on the frame first to cover the bare wood and create a richly-coloured base against which the pale driftwood will really show to its best advantage.

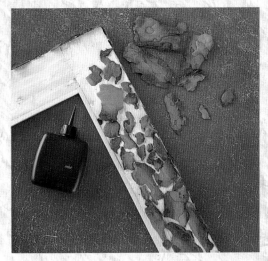

1. Cover one of the outer edges of the frame with clear adhesive, then stick small flakes of bark to it to cover the bare wood. Allow the glue to dry, then repeat with the other sides in turn to create an outer rim of bark.

2. Spread clear adhesive over the face of the frame and cover with larger flakes of bark, arranging them in mosaic fashion to cover as much of the bare wood as possible. Allow the glue to dry.

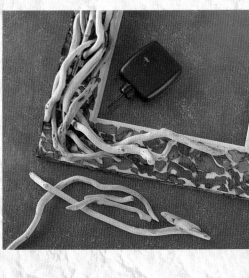

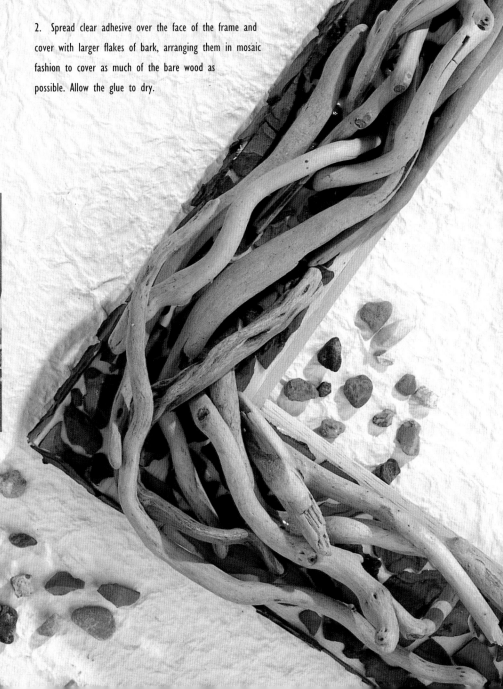

3. Choose the longest pieces of driftwood first and glue in position on the frame. Add more and more driftwood to build up a tangled effect, saving the smaller and more interesting pieces until last.

PRESSED LEAVES

Enjoy the beauty of nature by decorating a frame with pressed leaves. There are many beautiful shapes and colours to choose from and you may even like to experiment with delicate sprigs of dried herbs, many of which have very pretty leaf shapes. The leaves you choose will depend on the time of year, your personal preference and the picture you are framing.

Pressing leaves is simple and you don't really need to use a special press. Instead, carefully arrange the leaves in between two sheets of tissue or blotting paper. Slip the paper in between the pages of a heavy book and stand the book on an even surface. Pile more books on top for added weight. You should find that the leaves are pressed and ready to use within two to three weeks, depending on their size.

The leaves can be added to a plain wooden frame for a natural look or to a painted base like the one here. This frame has been painted with a mid green base coat, then ragged with a darker green to evoke the warm mossy hues of the forest.

1. Paint the back of each red leaf using a strong adhesive which dries to a clear finish. A pair of tweezers can be used to hold the leaf steady. Gently position each leaf onto the frame and press down firmly, taking care not to damage it.

2. Snip the green leaves into small pieces. Paint patches of thinned PVA glue between the red leaves and press the green leaves into position on the wet glue. Paint over the leaves with more glue solution, mopping up any excess with kitchen paper.

3. When the glue is dry, paint the entire frame with one or two coats of satin finish varnish to seal any loose edges and protect the delicate leaves. Raise the frame off the work surface while you varnish it to prevent it from sticking.

59

SEED MOSAIC

The varied colours, shapes and sizes of dried seeds and beans make them an ideal medium for creating stunning mosaic patterns. Health food shops and supermarkets stock a varied selection from bright orange, green and yellow lentils to rich deep red kidney beans and delicate petal-shaped pumpkin seeds. Smaller seeds such as the black poppy seeds and white sesame seeds used here are also very effective, creating a denser, more even pattern.

The seeds can be combined to create interesting textures and patterns and, if varnished with several coats of gloss varnish, they can even be given the appearance of glass. Use an aerosol varnish if possible, to prevent the seeds being knocked off with a brush.

The frame you choose for this method should be fairly plain as it can be difficult to glue seeds over ridges and curves. It is a decorative technique in itself which benefits from having flat planes to show off the design to best advantage.

The frame needs to be coated with a good thick layer of adhesive to ensure that the seeds stick firmly. You may find it less messy to place the frame over a box or tin whilst sprinkling on the seeds as this makes it easy to collect the excess and re-use them.

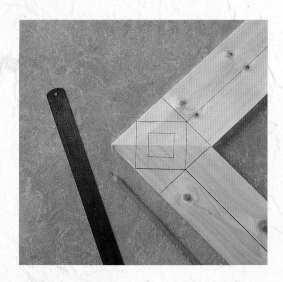

1. Draw your design onto the frame using a ruler and soft pencil. Apply a coat of glue to one area at a time and sprinkle on the seeds, pressing down firmly with your palm. Use a ruler to nudge the seeds into a straight edge where necessary.

2. Shake off any loose seeds then go on to the next section using the same colour. Any gaps can be filled later by painting glue onto the bare areas and sprinkling on extra seeds once the rest of the pattern has dried.

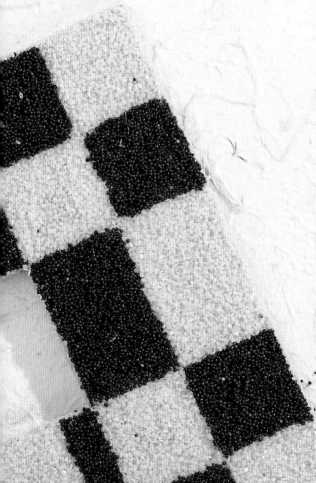

3. When all the sections of one colour are complete, repeat the process using the next colour and continue in this way until the entire frame is covered, including the edges. When the glue is dry, apply two thin coats of varnish to the frame.

ROUND ROPE FRAME

This is a very easy frame to make: all you need is a disk of plywood, some rope or cord and strong glue. There is such a huge range of ropes and cords available in a good selection of different widths and colours that you can create lots of different effects. You could mix two or more different types, as we have with the frame on the left, or use just one type of rope as we have with the frame below. These frames look particularly good when framing a mirror.

Circles of rope are glued on to a thin plywood disk, which can either be purchased ready-cut, or can be cut at home if you can't find the right size. Measure your mirror or picture and draw a circle on the plywood disk to show how much space to leave for it. When all the rope rings are in place around the frame, fit the mirror or picture and glass into the centre, holding it in place with panel pins knocked in at 45° around the edges. Add a last ring of rope inside the others to hide the edges of the glass or mirror.

1. Use a pencil to mark a circle in the middle of the plywood to show the size of your mirror or artwork. Cut the first ring of rope to fit around this line, splicing the ends between twists so they fit together neatly.

2. Lay a thick bed of strong glue along the pencil line and position the ring of rope on top, securing it in place at intervals using panel pins. Repeat with increasingly longer pieces of rope to cover the plywood right to the edge.

3. Cut lengths of thinner rope for decoration and glue between the thicker pieces as required. Position the artwork or mirror, using glue or pins to secure, then stick a circle of thin rope around the inside of the frame to hide the edges.

FRAYED HESSIAN

This simple idea can be easily adapted to suit your own taste or requirements. I have chosen hessian because of its rustic, country feel and because it frays easily, being fairly open weave, but you could choose any fabric you like. If you feel it is not suitable for your picture or the room in which you intend to hang it, try using lace instead. This would create a very pretty, bedroom style frame, which could be finished with matching beads or buttons in the corners.

The frames here were covered with ordinary giftwrapping paper before the hessian was added. You could, however, stick the hessian decoration on a bare wood frame or cover the frame with patterned or plain fabric, wallpaper, crêpe or tissue first.

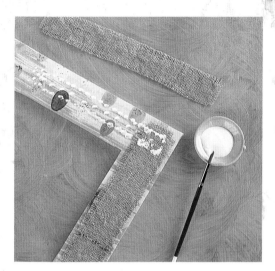

1. Cut four strips of hessian slightly narrower and shorter than the sides of your frame. Fray the edges of each piece to create a narrow fringe all round, by pulling out one thread at a time until you are happy with the result.

2. Glue the hessian strips onto the frame, positioning the short lengths first with the ends of the longer lengths lying on top. Apply the glue to the main fabric only, leaving the frayed edges loose.

3. Cut four small squares of hessian and four larger squares of muslin for corner decorations. The muslin looks more effective if it is cut slightly off-square. Fray the edges of each piece of fabric.

4. Glue a muslin square onto each corner of your frame and then glue a frayed hessian square on top. Complete each corner by gluing a star anise to the centre of the hessian detail.

PEBBLE & MOSS FRAME

A collage of natural objects collected from the beach or from a forest adds a stylish focal point to any wall. This bleached wood frame is decorated with pebbles and reindeer moss and makes an ideal surround for a nature collection, like the one shown on page 11, It is a rather dominant frame, by its size alone, but this is reduced by making the frame part of the overall image, continuing the seaside theme from the collage. It would also be perfect as a nautical mirror frame to suit any room in the house from the bathroom to the bedroom.

The pebbles here have been gathered from the beach and have a beautiful smooth, rounded shape which contrasts well with the rough, lacy texture of the reindeer moss. Using stones of a similar size creates a pleasing balanced border which allows the individual markings and subtle colour changes in each stone to shine through.

Reindeer moss can be purchased from florists or garden centres and it is available in a wide variety of colours which enables you choose the right shade to match your pebbles.

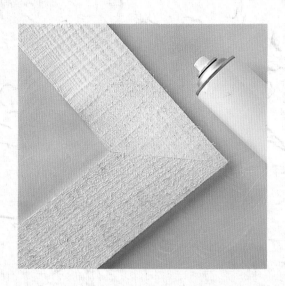

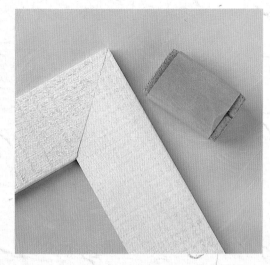

1. Paint the rough wood frame with a thin, even coat of white paint. The colour should not be too dense and it is important to achieve an even coverage. Spray paint is ideal for creating this light look. Allow the paint to dry.

2. Sand the frame using medium grained sandpaper to remove any rough edges and surfaces. The natural colour of the wood will begin to show through the paint layer. Apply a second thin coat of paint and sand again when dry.

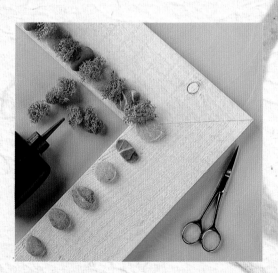

3. Arrange a pattern of pebbles along the inner edge of the frame, spacing them evenly. Use a strong adhesive to glue them into position. Cut small pieces of reindeer moss and glue these in between the pebbles.

PAINTED STARFISH

This colourful frame is made by sticking starfish and shells onto a rough wood frame using tile adhesive. White, blue and green paints are then applied to the frame and shells to create this lively, distressed effect. The blue and green colours are painted over the white basecoat, then the excess is removed with a rag. This creates a broken finish, leaving the majority of the colour in the wood grain and shell recesses. This is why it is important to start with a rough, rather than a smooth, wooden frame.

If you are not lucky enough to find starfish washed up on the beach, you can find them quite easily in craft or gift shops. They are usually available in many different sizes, so you will be able to select the best ones to fit your frame. Shells can be easily found in all shapes and sizes, and although the frame we have made here is quite simple, you could use the same method to add many more shells and starfish to create a fuller pattern. The advantage of using shells is that each has its own pretty shape and it is not difficult to make an attractive arrangement with them.

1. Stick the starfish and shells to the frame with tile adhesive. Make sure there are no gaps around the edges, packing in extra adhesive where needed. Allow to dry, then sand down any big lumps of excess adhesive on the frame.

2. Paint the frame white, making sure you cover the starfish and shells thoroughly. I have used a white acrylic spray paint which gives an even coverage right into all the cracks and crevices in the shells.

3. Lightly paint the entire frame bright blue using a thinned water-based paint. Remove the excess paint with a rag, allow to dry, then repeat with a sea green paint to leave a distressed effect. Once dry, apply one or two coats of varnish.

SEASHELL FRAME

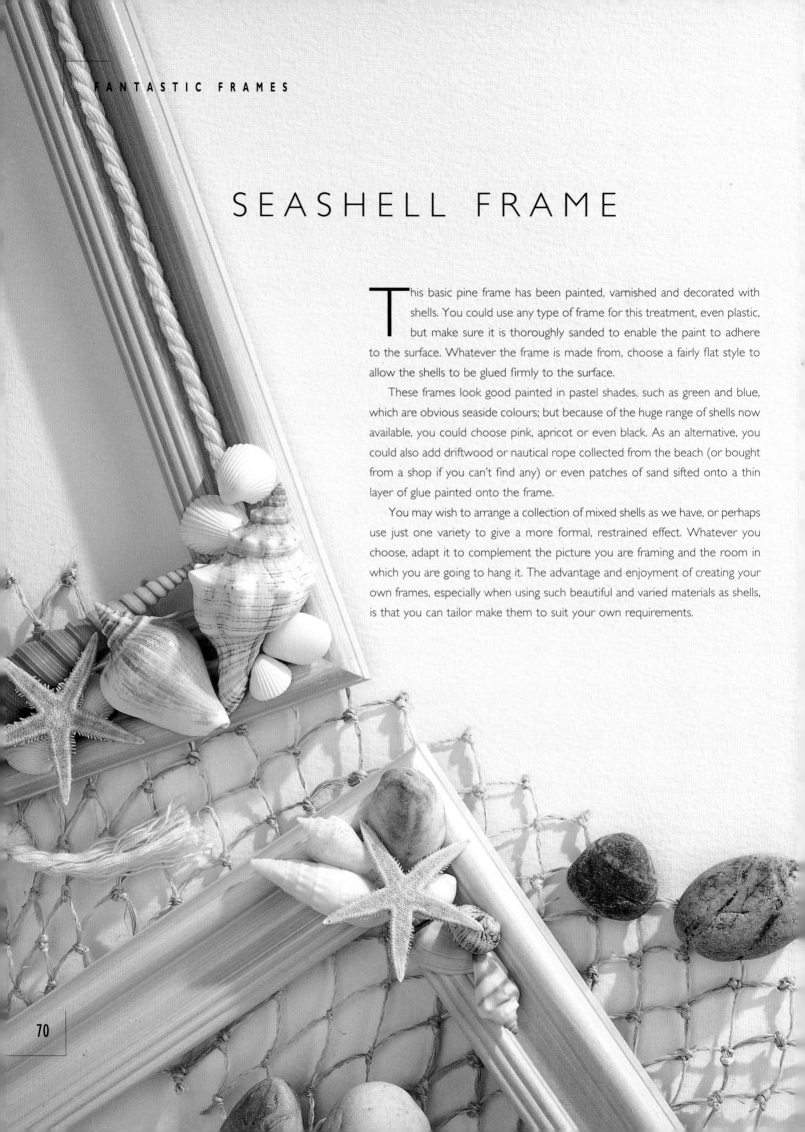

This basic pine frame has been painted, varnished and decorated with shells. You could use any type of frame for this treatment, even plastic, but make sure it is thoroughly sanded to enable the paint to adhere to the surface. Whatever the frame is made from, choose a fairly flat style to allow the shells to be glued firmly to the surface.

These frames look good painted in pastel shades, such as green and blue, which are obvious seaside colours; but because of the huge range of shells now available, you could choose pink, apricot or even black. As an alternative, you could also add driftwood or nautical rope collected from the beach (or bought from a shop if you can't find any) or even patches of sand sifted onto a thin layer of glue painted onto the frame.

You may wish to arrange a collection of mixed shells as we have, or perhaps use just one variety to give a more formal, restrained effect. Whatever you choose, adapt it to complement the picture you are framing and the room in which you are going to hang it. The advantage and enjoyment of creating your own frames, especially when using such beautiful and varied materials as shells, is that you can tailor make them to suit your own requirements.

1. Lightly sand the frame with a fine grade paper to ensure the paint will adhere to it, particularly if it is an old frame or has been treated with varnish, wax or paint. Using either a brush or aerosol, paint the frame white and allow to dry.

2. Thin some green emulsion with water and apply to one side of the frame at a time. Before the paint dries, drag the surface with a dry brush to create an uneven, striped effect. Wipe the brush with a clean rag between strokes. Allow to dry.

3. Use a fine brush and more of the emulsion to paint a fine line in each recess in the frame to emphasise its shape. Before the lines dry, lightly wipe over them with a clean rag to soften the effect. Apply two coats of varnish to protect the paint.

4. Use a strong adhesive to glue the shells to the frame. Start with the larger shells to create the basic shape, then add smaller ones to build up the design. You could either stick shells all around the frame or just limit them to the corners.

PAINTED BEAN FRAME

Dried beans, peas and lentils can be used to create interesting surface texture on a frame. Rather than varnishing them to create a natural look, these pulses have been painted so they are not instantly recognised for what they are, but instead become more abstract forms. The frame here is reminiscent of early bakelite mouldings.

There is a huge selection of different beans now available and each has its own individual shape. The beans can be arranged in a wide variety of patterns to suit personal taste. A strong glue should be used to hold the pulses firmly in place to create a hard-wearing frame as this frame remains unvarnished and there is no final protective glazing. The beans themselves are surprisingly tough and you should find that your finished frame can take general day to day wear and tear without any problems.

We have painted the frame in a dull red and spattered black gloss paint over the top for a speckled finish. You could, of course, paint your frame any colour you like, but it will look most effective if you spatter a different shade over the top to break up the base colour.

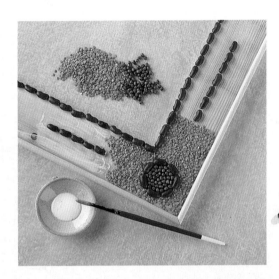

1. Using a strong adhesive, stick a row of red kidney beans along the inner edge of the frame to create a border. Glue a ring of beans in each corner and a short row of beans down the centre of each of the frame sides.

2. Glue mung beans into each of the four circles, pressing them into place until each circle is filled. When dry, apply a coat of glue to the remaining bare areas and sprinkle on lentils, pressing them into place and shaking off any excess.

3. When the glue is thoroughly dry, paint the entire frame and all the beans using red matt spray paint. Apply the paint in several thin coats, turning the frame between each coat to achieve an even finish.

4. Paint the outside edge of the frame using black gloss. Thin some of the black paint according to the manufacturer's instructions and spatter over the frame by flicking the paint brush bristles.

DECOUPAGE CHERUBS

Découpage is a popular and effective way of decorating not only frames, but also boxes, trays and furniture of any sort. The technique involves cutting patterns and motifs from pieces of paper and using them to decorate the surface of an object. Varnish is then applied to seal and protect the design.

The effects you can attain are endless and varied as you can use all sorts of different papers: wallpaper, pages from books or magazines, giftwrapping paper or sheet music, as we have here. It is also possible to buy special sheets of découpage paper in a range of different designs from craft suppliers. The only consideration when choosing the paper is that it should not be too thick if you want to maintain a smooth surface on the frame.

The design will be most effective if you only partially cover the frame with découpage, allowing the gold and copper tones of the paint to show through from underneath. Here we started off with some strips of sheet music, then glued some gold cherubs and other motifs cut from a sheet of giftwrapping paper over the top to carry on the classical theme. You could, of course, choose any motifs you like, perhaps reflecting the theme of the picture you are framing. Whatever you choose, make sure you give the finished frame at least two coats of varnish to give it a deep lustre.

1. Paint the frame white using eggshell or spray paint. Thin a little gold, acrylic paint with water and apply unevenly with a damp sponge, wiping over the flat surfaces and dabbing on the curved areas. Be sure to apply it to the corners and recesses.

2. Thin some copper, acrylic paint and apply on top in the same way when the gold is dry, this time using a fine brush in the recesses. While it is drying, cut wavy strips from a sheet of music and carefully cut the cherubs from the paper.

3. Glue the sheet music strips to the frame, trimming the ends to fit neatly into the recesses. Leave gaps between the strips to allow the paint to show. Glue the cherubs over the music strips in a continuous pattern around the frame.

4. When the glue is thoroughly dry, paint the frame with an ageing varnish to give it a rich, deep finish. You will probably need to apply two coats to seal the frame completely and prevent the paper pieces peeling off.

CHUNKY PAPIER MACHE

Papier mâché is a very simple technique to master, and this cheerful, chunky frame requires very little artistic ability at all. The frame has been painted with a very simple effect, applied with kitchen paper and a rag. The motifs are torn from giftwrapping paper and pieces of purple tissue are stuck on top.

The only disadvantage with papier mâché is the overnight drying time needed between each layer of paper, but this frame can be made in a morning if you use a microwave to speed things up. Each time the frame has to dry, place in a microwave on a high setting for one minute and you should find the paste has dried thoroughly, allowing you to apply another layer immediately.

If you want to create a sleeve into which to slide the picture, lay an extra rectangle of card behind the papier mâché covered frame and join the two together by sticking strips of newspaper over the join on three sides, leaving one side open. Apply another layer when the first has dried. Then carry on with decorating the frame, as described in the instructions.

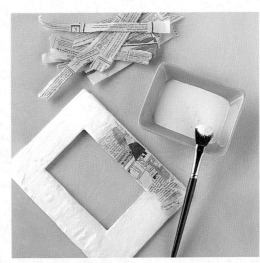

1. Cut a frame from either mountboard or card, making it slightly wider at the bottom than at the top or sides. Brush the frame all over with wallpaper paste. While this is drying, tear some strips of newspaper for papier mâché.

2. Stick a layer of newspaper strips onto the frame until covered, using wallpaper paste. Leave to dry overnight, then paste on two more layers in the same way, allowing to dry thoroughly between each. Paint the frame with white emulsion.

3. Thin some white emulsion, dip a piece of scrunched kitchen paper into it and dab on the frame sparingly. Repeat with green paint while the white is wet. Thin some pink water colour and wipe on the frame with a rag to create irregular patches.

4. When the paint is dry, tear some motifs roughly from sheets of giftwrapping paper and paste on to the frame. Paste pieces of torn purple tissue on top, some creased, some overlapping the motifs. When dry, apply two coats of varnish.

CROCKERY MOSAIC

If you have ever wanted to know what to do with those old odd plates, cups and saucers, well here is the answer. A very easy and fun frame to make which costs very little. These frames have a bright, bold look which would make them suitable for hanging in the kitchen, but you could create any style you like by varying the colour and shape of the beading and the type of crockery used. For example, a very smart frame could be made using only willow pattern crockery, perhaps with a shaped beading around the edges coloured with a dark wood stain. This frame would look good in a dining room. You could co-ordinate your mosaic to match the picture you are framing or the room you are hanging it in, especially if you are framing a mirror.

As you become more confident, you may wish to create shapes within the mosaic, such as a flower. You would need to lay out the shape first and then continue with the mosaic around it, perhaps using a contrasting colour to make the pattern really show.

1. To create a raised edge for the mosaic, pin thin, square beading along all outer edges of the frame, cutting the pieces to the lengths required. Repeat with all inner edges so you are left with a wide channel on all four sides.

2. Choose a selection of chipped crockery from charity shops or from your own kitchen. Lay the pieces under a piece of cardboard and smash them with a hammer. The cardboard will prevent the pieces flying up.

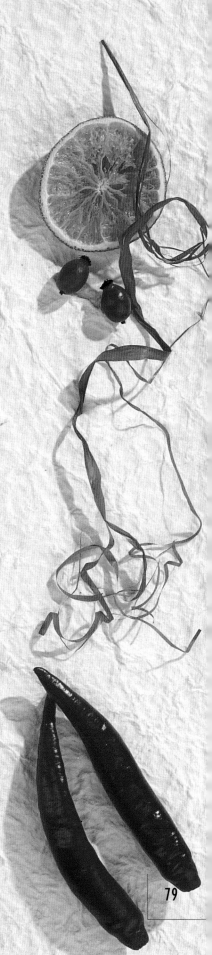

3. Fill the frame with tile adhesive to just below the top of the beading. Choose some pieces of crockery with straight edges and push them into the adhesive, butting them up against the beading. Fill in the gaps with other suitably-shaped pieces.

4. When the mosaic is complete, wipe over the surface of the pieces with a damp cloth to remove any smudges of adhesive. Leave to dry. Paint the beading with a suitable colour to complement your selection of crockery.

PUNCHED TIN

Punched tin is, in many countries, a form of folk art. In America, it is believed to have originated from the Dutch immigrants and was practised by tinkers and other craftsmen to decorate furniture and household items. This frame is made from sheets of tin punched with traditional folk art shapes such as hearts. The tin is pinned onto a basic wood frame. You could punch tin with any shapes or designs you choose, but if you want to create a folk art look, stick to hearts, stars, diamonds and tulips. Whatever you choose, simple shapes will look most effective.

You can buy thin sheet tin from metal merchants, and most sell it in small pieces. Another source, however, is to use old tin cans. Just wash them and cut them up with tin snips or strong scissors and hammer out the corrugations if there are any. The only disadvantage with recycling tin cans is that they are not very big, but this is not a problem if you don't mind having joins in your tin work - it can actually look quite interesting.

1. Measure your frame and draw its outline onto graph paper. Draw your design in the space within the frame, leaving a narrow margin along all the edges where the pins will go. Cut out the paper shapes you have drawn.

2. Wearing protective gloves, cut out the tin frame and file away any sharp edges. Lay the paper templates on the wrong side of the tin and draw around them using an indelible pen. Draw a line just in from each edge, and any extra detail.

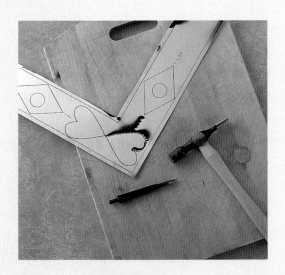

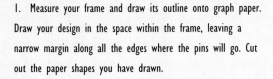

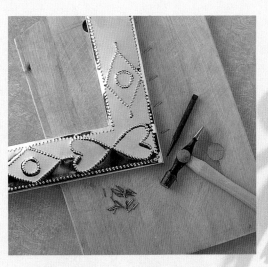

3. Lay the tin frame onto a sturdy board and, using either a nail or a centre punch, hammer a series of indentations along the pen marks. Keep the punch marks evenly spaced and strike the punch the same amount of times when making each mark.

4. Turn the tin over and lay it in position on the wooden frame. Holding it firmly in place, tack the tin facade onto the frame inserting tacks along both the inner and outer edges. If the frame is deep, tack strips of tin around the outside edges.

WIRE MESH SCROLLS

This unusual frame is made by applying papier mâché over wire mesh shapes stapled onto a basic wooden frame. The wire mesh creates an interesting honeycomb effect under the papier mâché, giving the frame an unusual finish. The colours and shapes of this frame were inspired by the sea, which can be seen in the curved edges and the use of pearlised and blue paints.

Papier mâché is a simple technique which can be used to create a range of varying effects, depending on the type of paper you use, how many layers you apply and the way in which you paint it. Rather than the usual newspaper, the papier mâché on this frame was made using much thicker paper from a paperback book, which creates a more uneven surface.

You can adapt this technique of making the frame to suit your own needs, whether you want to make a surreal frame like this one, or a colourful, chunky frame using thicker papier mâché and bright primary paints.

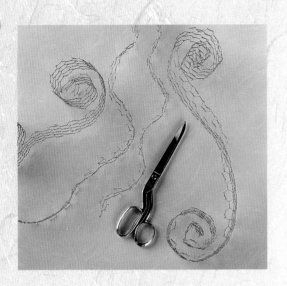

1. Cut two thin strips of wire mesh one and a half times the height of the frame and bend into a series of smooth waves. Next cut two wider strips about twice the width of the frame and curl each end into a scroll. Tuck in any sharp edges.

2. Use a staple gun to fix the wavy pieces to the two sides of the frame to create shaped edges. Next staple the two scrolls onto the front of the frame, arranged horizontally top and bottom. Hammer in the staples if the wood is very hard.

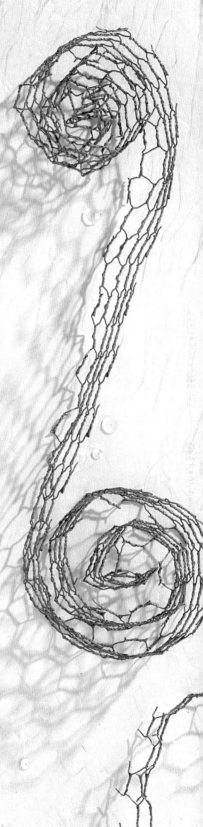

3. Mix up a small quantity of wallpaper paste. Tear the paper into strips and dip them into the paste, one by one. Position the strips on the frame, being sure to cover all surfaces, both horizontal and vertical. Leave to dry overnight and repeat.

4. When completely dry, spray the frame white, applying as many coats as necessary to cover the print. Hand paint random patches of powder blue and pearl blue acrylic paints, defining the scrolls and the torn edges of the paper pieces.

SCRUNCHED TISSUE

Scrunched tissue is a simple but effective material with which to decorate a frame. The tissue is scrunched up, stuck on the frame and then spray painted; it really couldn't be easier. You can use the technique to create a new frame, as we have, or you could decorate an existing frame to give it a new lease of life. The advantage of this idea is that the scrunched tissue can be stuck onto either flat or bevelled surfaces. You can vary the effect by varying the size of the strips of tissue you scrunch up. Why not experiment before you begin to see what effects you can create? Aerosol paint will give the most even finish and will allow you to get paint into all the creases in the tissue if you regularly vary the direction from which you are spraying. An alternative is to use tissue of the colour you want your frame to be so you will not have to paint at all. If you decide to use more than one colour, plan the frame carefully first to achieve a balanced effect.

1. Tear some small strips of tissue and lightly scrunch them. Paint glue onto the frame, an area at a time, and stick the scrunched tissue to it, pressing the pieces down firmly and making sure there are no loose ends.

2. Continue until the whole frame is covered with tissue. Then make a dome for each of the corners by screwing a piece of tissue into a ball and covering it with another layer of tissue to make a smooth surface. Glue in place.

3. Use an aerosol paint to spray the frame in gold, making sure you get paint into all the creases and crevices. You may need to apply more than one coat of paint, so follow the manufacturer's instructions.

4. When the gold paint is thoroughly dry, use a contrasting colour for the corner domes. We have used copper acrylic paint to maintain the metallic theme; silver would also be a good choice with gold.

RUSTIC STENCILS

This frame has been made using recycled pallet board wood, which has a nice rough, rustic look. It is quite chunky and lends itself well to this kind of treatment. Instead of creating neat mitred corners, just cut four pieces of the same length with straight ends. Lay them right sides down on a firm surface to form a square and staple together with heavy-duty staples.

The frame has been stencilled with simple, country-style designs which fit in well with the roughness of the finish. Stencilling is basically a simple technique, but you may want to practise a little first on a piece of scrap paper. Use a paint brush or sponge and apply the paint sparingly. Always remove some of the paint on a scrap of paper before applying to the stencil; this way you can build up the colour in thin layers without it bleeding onto the wood. Stencils are easy to make, so why not design one that reflects the picture you are framing? Or maybe one to match the furnishing fabric in the room you intend to hang it in? This frame would also make an attractive mirror surround.

1. Paint the frame cream, then sand down to remove splinters. Draw the vine design on tracing paper, then transfer onto stencil card and cut out using a sharp craft knife. Cut a series of triangles and a thin strip out of another piece of stencil card.

2. Use well-diluted paints to create a wide beige stripe round the middle of the flat surface, and a finer green stripe around the outer edge and sides. Line up the second stencil and sponge on green paint to create a line of triangles along the inner edge.

3. While the paint dries, use masking tape to cover the berries on the vine stencil. Position the stencil over the beige stripe and sponge dark green paint sparingly over the stencil to create the vine stem and leaves. Move the stencil and continue.

4. Remove the masking tape and reposition the stencil on the frame, using the stems to line it up. Sponge red paint over the berries. Use the stencil strip to create a red border between the vine and the triangles. Apply clear, matt varnish to seal.

PAPER SHAPES

Stained glass windows have always held a fascination for me, with their pure colours and the way the patterns are made from a series of perfectly fitting parts, surrounded by lead. It is this which inspired me to create a frame to reflect that style, by the use of handmade papers and thick acrylic outline.

I used handmade rather than machine produced papers because of their textures and inherent imperfections which make them more interesting. These particular papers have sparkling silver threads in them which seem to make the colours richer and more luxurious.

You could choose any combination of colours to suit your needs, but if you want to retain the stained glass effect you will need to stick to strong, pure tones. You could abandon the stained glass idea altogether, though, and use the same technique with a selection of papers of varying natural or pastel shades for a completely different effect. As with any of these paper projects, you could use fabric instead. If you choose to, I would suggest using an iron-on backing which gives the fabric more substance and prevents it from fraying.

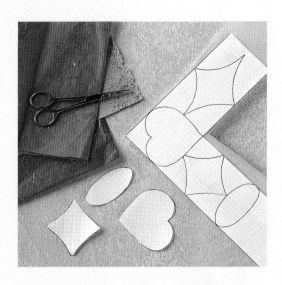

1. Make a template of the frame on graph paper and draw out your design. Cut out the design elements and use as templates to cut the shapes from handmade papers. Cut out a rectangle of handmade paper slightly bigger than the frame.

2. Spread thinned PVA glue on the front of the frame then lay it, face down, on the rectangle of paper. Cut out the centre, leaving a turning all round. Cut the corners as shown, then paste all edges up the sides and on to the back of the frame.

3. Patch up the gaps in the inside corners with extra paper, then give the whole frame a coat of thinned PVA and allow to dry. Glue the handmade paper shapes in place then coat again with thinned PVA glue, sealing all loose edges.

4. When the glue is thoroughly dry, use gold acrylic paint to outline the shapes and the edges of the frame. While it is still wet, use a thin stick to distress the acrylic and make it resemble beaten metal.

NAUTICAL FRAME

Corrugated card is now available in a variety of colours and is very easy to use. The navy and royal blue shades have a rather smart, nautical feel which inspired this frame. The frame facade is made from two layers of corrugated card: royal blue underneath and navy on top. The navy layer is slighter shorter and has a porthole cut into it, allowing the royal blue to show from underneath. The frame is trimmed with bright white cord and decorated with white corrugated card wave shapes top and bottom. Corrugated card should be cut, flat side up, with a craft knife to ensure the corrugations are cut neatly. It is an interesting idea to use areas of card with the corrugations lying in different directions; you may want to incorporate this in your design. If you are using this frame in a bathroom, make it from corrugated plastic instead.

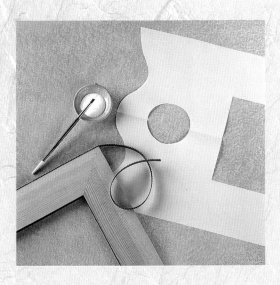

1. Using the frame as a template, draw your design onto paper and cut out. Cut out the centre window and the circular porthole. Cut strips of paper the same depth as your frame and glue onto the inside and outside edges of the frame.

2. Lay the pattern on the royal blue paper, draw round it and cut out. Do not cut out the circle. Trim a margin from the top of the paper pattern. Lay the revised pattern onto the navy paper, draw round it and cut out, including the circle.

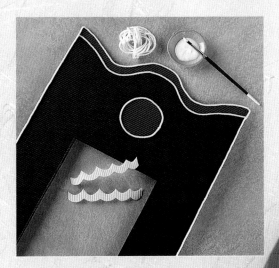

3. Stick strips of double-sided tape along the back of the navy paper shape. Peel off the backing strips and gently lower the navy paper shape onto the larger royal blue shape, taking care to align all the edges. Press the two pieces together.

4. Glue the paper facade to the frame. When dry, stick white cord around the circle, and along the wavy top edges. Continue along the inner and outer edges of the frame. Cut wavy lines from white corrugated paper and glue into position.

GINGHAM HEARTS

The combination of gingham fabric with cross stitch decoration and folk art shapes gives this frame a traditional crafted look reminiscent of the simple lines of Shaker style. The elongated hearts are a traditional motif of this timeless, yet fashionable, style. It is an adaptable look which works well in all rooms from the kitchen to the bedroom.

A small frame in this style is perfect for displaying photographs. A cardboard backing can be attached to the reverse of the frame using strips of sticky tape running down the two sides and along the bottom. A photograph can then be slipped into the open top.

The frame makes use of four different colours of gingham, one for each side of the frame. The four pieces are cut out and joined by sticking them onto a piece of iron-on interfacing. The motifs and stitches are then applied and the whole thing is glued onto the card frame. The excess fabric along the inner and outer edges is turned over to the back of the frame and glued in place.

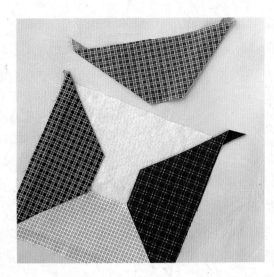

1. Cut a square frame from cardboard using a craft knife. Draw diagonal lines through two adjacent corners and trace off the resulting shape to make a pattern. Cut out the shape from each type of gingham adding a small seam allowance all round.

2. Lay the template on the wrong side of the gingham and press the diagonal sides over. Lay the four pieces face-up on the interfacing with the wrong sides in contact with the glue. Butt the edges together to form a square and iron in place.

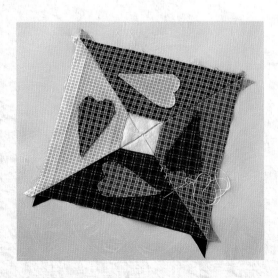

3. Make a heart template and draw round it onto the backing paper of the interfacing four times. Cut out the shapes and iron onto gingham. Cut out the hearts leaving extra to turn over. Snip the fabric up to the backing paper; press the turnings over.

4. Iron the hearts in place. Cross stitch each seam and around the hearts. Sew a button on each heart. Cut out the centre of the interfacing and snip down the seams slightly. Glue the fabric to the card frame, turning over the inner and outer edges.

GINGERBREAD MEN

Salt dough is simple to make and extremely versatile. The soft dough can be manipulated into many shapes and can be treated in much the same way as pastry, using cutters and templates to make neat edges. You could make the frame any shape you like and decorate with any kinds of motifs - perhaps fruit shapes or flowers, or even a favourite cartoon character for a child's bedroom. The shapes do not have to be flat like our gingerbread men; they can be three-dimensional as long as they are firmly attached to the frame.

The basic salt dough recipe is as follows: 8oz (200g) plain flour, 8oz (200g) salt, about 1/4 pint (1/8 litre) warm water, 1 tbsp oil, 1 tbsp reconstituted wallpaper paste (optional). The dough is made by mixing all the dry ingredients together in a bowl and then adding water a little at a time to form a firm, flexible paste. The salt dough should be baked in a low oven (100°C/250°F/gas mark 1/2) until it is completely dry and hard.

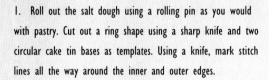

1. Roll out the salt dough using a rolling pin as you would with pastry. Cut out a ring shape using a sharp knife and two circular cake tin bases as templates. Using a knife, mark stitch lines all the way around the inner and outer edges.

2. Roll out the dough offcuts and cut out six gingerbread men. Mark the eyes and noses with a skewer and the mouths using a cutter. Slide all the pieces onto a baking tray lined with silicone paper and bake for 3-4 hours until completely dry.

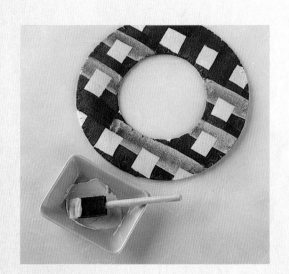

3. When the frame has cooled, paint a check pattern on it using blue acrylic. Allow to dry. Thin yellow acrylic with water and paint a yellow check on top and stitches around the edges. Paint the gingerbread men's eyes blue and pencil in the mouths.

4. Paint nine small buttons blue and a further nine yellow. Glue three buttons to the front of each man, then glue the men in position on the frame. Apply varnish to the back of the frame, allow to dry, then varnish the front thoroughly.

PAINTED CLIP FRAME

A clip frame is an easy and economical way to frame a picture, protecting the picture and allowing it to be hung on a wall in the usual way. The disadvantage, however, is that it will not create any additional decoration or boundary between the picture and the wall. One way to remedy this is to use glass paints to decorate the glass in the frame.

Start by designing a pattern on a piece of paper, but remember to refer to the picture you are framing to make sure you leave enough room for it to show through - you don't want your pattern encroaching on the picture. You then slip the pattern behind the glass and copy it onto the glass using relief outline which is made for this purpose. It creates a raised edge which will contain the runny glass paint when it is applied. Make sure you don't leave any gaps in the relief outline or the glass paint will leak through.

The relief outline and glass paint can be applied to either the back or front of the glass, giving different effects. If you apply it to the front, as we have, you may find that the clips that hold the frame together will mark the paint, so will always have to be kept in the same positions.

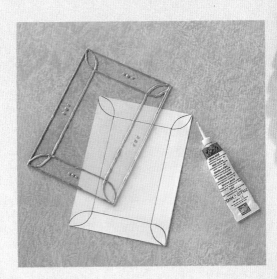

1. Draw around the glass from the frame onto a piece of paper to make a rectangle. Mark out an area for the frame inside the shape you have drawn and draw your design within this area, adding all pattern details.

2. Clean the glass with vinegar and warm water to remove any dirt and grease. Place the glass on top of your design and, using gold relief outline, draw onto the glass following the lines of the design below to create a thin, raised line.

3. Allow the outline to dry thoroughly, then fill the spaces in the design with coloured glass paints. Apply the paints in one thick coat as evenly as possible to create a smooth, dense stained glass effect.

FELT MOTIF FRAME

This colourful felt frame is ideal for a child's room, especially if used to frame a mirror. Its bold shapes and vivid colours would brighten up any wall and you could choose colours to match the decoration in the room. It would be a nice idea to include the child's name in the design, or maybe the shape of a favourite animal or pet.

The basic wooden frame is covered with a layer of wadding to pad out the felt and give it a nice rounded appearance. The wadding is cut to the same shape as the frame, just a little wider on all sides. Felt is a very easy material to work with, and if applied carefully, the glue won't seep through it to the front. You could, therefore, get your child to help make the frame by cutting out the shapes and sticking them on. This is great fun and you will have a very individual and personal frame at the end of it.

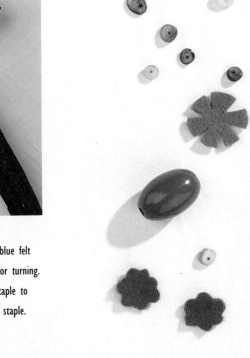

1. Cut wadding and lay on frame. Cut squares of felt for the corners, with extra to turn over. Staple the outer edges of the squares to the back of the frame, cut a slit in each inside corner, pull taut and staple the points to the frame back.

2. Cut two pieces of orange felt and two pieces of blue felt to fit the frame sides, allowing extra on the widths for turning. Lay each felt strip over one side of the frame and staple to the back. Pull the felt taut over the wadding as you staple.

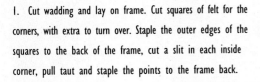

3. Cut four strips of pink felt and cut a wavy line down the centre of each. Glue the strips to the frame with a small gap between the two pieces. Cut rectangles, spirals and zigzag shapes in different colours and use to decorate the frame.

4. Back four rectangles of fabric with iron-on interfacing. Remove the backing and iron the shapes into place, following the manufacturer's instructions. Using fabric paints, add some decorative details such as circles, crosses and hearts as shown.

STRIPED DECOUPAGE

This economical frame decoration looks effective and is also a great way to use up scraps of giftwrap or to recycle glossy magazines. The basic frame is covered with strips of torn paper which are overlapped and glued into place. You do not have to be fussy about what is printed on the paper, as the overall effect is one of an abstract design of shape and colour.

It is easy to create different looks by varying the widths of the paper strips and the colour combinations. You may choose to use a wide mixture of colours and shapes or limit your palette to create a subtle frame which harmonises with the picture inside. Another idea is to use two alternating colours to create a stripy, zebra effect.

All manner of frame shapes are suitable for this technique as the flexible paper can be eased into any grooves and ridges while the glue is still wet. Once the glue has dried, the paper can be sealed with polyurethane varnish to give it a tough protective finish. You will need to apply two coats of varnish, leaving the first to dry before applying the second coat.

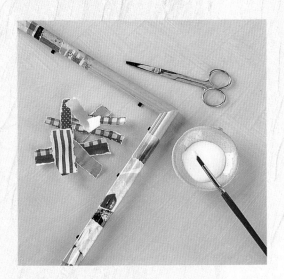

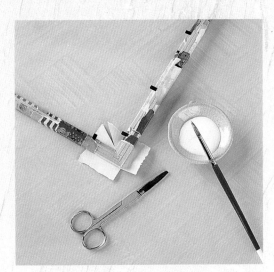

1. Tear some sheets of brightly coloured, glossy paper into strips of varying widths. Glue the strips around the frame, overlapping them at the edges until you reach the corner. Use a closed pair of scissors to ease the paper into the moulding.

2. Tear a large rectangle of paper for each corner. Glue it to the front of the frame. Cut a square from the paper at the outside edge of the frame and a diagonal slit on the inside. Glue the remaining tabs to the back of the frame.

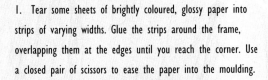

3. When the glue is thoroughly dry, apply two thin coats of varnish, allowing it to dry completely between coats. The varnish will seal any loose edges of paper and create a tough, protective finish for the frame.

PADDED FABRIC FRAME

One of the good things about this frame is that it can be decorated with all manner of items which are associated with the picture you are framing. For example, you could embroider a name or date on the frame if you choose a plain rather than a patterned fabric to cover it. You could stick on fabric shapes as decoration or decorate the fabric yourself with fabric paints. Another nice idea is to chose the fabric to match the curtains or other soft furnishings in the room in which you intend to hang the frame. You could also add lace, buttons or beads to create the effect you want.

Cut a layer of wadding, the same shape but slightly wider than the frame on all sides to fit between the fabric and frame, giving a softly padded effect. Any type of frame, new or old, is suitable for covering with fabric; it doesn't matter if it is shaped as it will just give the finished frame more shape.

If you intend to give the frame as a gift, or you would like a neat finish, you could cover the back of the frame too. Trim off any excess fabric and cover the back of the frame with a non-fray fabric such as felt, gluing it over the loose ends and hiding the staples.

1. Cut the wadding slightly wider than the frame and snip in the inner corners. Cut a piece of fabric to fit the frame, leaving a wide margin on all sides for fixing to the back. Lay the frame on top of the wadding, on top of the face-down fabric.

2. Fold all the outer edges of fabric up and over the back of the frame and staple in place. Start on one side, then pull the outer edge on the opposite side of the frame taut and staple that side next. Continue, folding the fabric in at the corners.

3. Make a neat diagonal snip running from each inner corner of the fabric to the inner corner of the frame. Pull the fabric taut to the back of the frame and staple all the inner edges in place in the same way as the outer edges.

4. To cover the raw corners, cut four rectangles of fabric. Gather the fabric, tucking under any raw edges. Stretch each over a corner, stapling it in place on the inner and outer edges of the back of the frame. Sew a button in each corner.

FANTASY PEARL FRAME

It is quite surprising how adaptable and useful wood filler can be. You can buy it ready mixed so you can be sure it will be the right consistency and will remain workable for a long time. This means you will have plenty of time to work your design. Remember to check the instructions on the packet as to the thickness achievable with the product you have purchased; if you make it too thick, it may crack.

This is a fun frame which should not be taken too seriously. You can make a random swirly pattern in the wood filler as we have, or you could make a more specific pattern of stripes, zigzags or circles, for example. Do not try anything too elaborate as the filler will probably be too coarse to hold an intricate pattern. You can, however, be as elaborate as you like with the decoration. We have made fantasy frames with shimmering paint, clear plastic beads in a variety of colours and strings of pearls. You could be far more sensible and paint the frame in a plain colour to match your decor, if you prefer.

1. Following the manufacturer's instructions, spread a thick coat of filler onto the front and the edges of the frame. Use a wooden stick to make swirls in the filler. You don't have to be too neat as any lumps can be sanded down later.

2. While the filler is still wet, use a spatula or small knife to create a narrow, flat surface along the inner edges of the front of the frame. Press the beads in position into the filler to create hollows and then remove them and leave the frame to dry.

3. When the filler has set, paint the frame using a water-based or spray paint. Any hairline cracks can be filled with paint. When the paint is dry, glue a string of pearls along the inner edge of the frame and glue the beads in place.

CHAPTER FIVE

DECORATIVE
MOUNTS

Mounts are usually used in plain colours with either a textured or flat surface, and you will find a huge range of commercial mountboard available, in every imaginable shade. Fine watercolour lines are traditionally used to decorate mounts, but it takes a great deal of skill to achieve a neat result. This section presents a range of alternative ideas which give a similar finish but which are much easier to do. There are also more unusual ideas for creating interesting mounts, from painting trompe l'oeil stonework to covering the mount in tartan paper. Whatever your requirements, mounts need never be plain again.

COLOUR WASHING

Colour washing is a popular and simple paint technique and a quick and effective way to decorate a mount. It doesn't take a great deal of skill to achieve an interesting finish. The most important pointer is to make sure the paint is of the right consistency. If it is too thick, it will not spread well on the mount and you will end up with a splodgy finish with dense patches of colour. On the other hand, if it is too thin, you could make the mountboard too wet and cause it to warp while it is drying.

You can experiment with alternative colours, perhaps picking out two shades from the picture you are mounting. You will get a more subtle effect the more similar the colours are, and a brighter effect the less alike they are. You can use pale colours for a softer look and deeper colours for a rich-toned mount which will create a very interesting border around a picture if used in the right circumstances. It is also possible to vary the depth of colour by using more coats of the same shades, or more than two different colours. Be careful, though: it is easy to end up with a murky mess by adding too much paint to the mount.

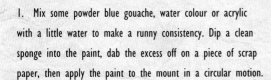

1. Mix some powder blue gouache, water colour or acrylic with a little water to make a runny consistency. Dip a clean sponge into the paint, dab the excess off on a piece of scrap paper, then apply the paint to the mount in a circular motion.

2. Allow the blue paint to dry, then thin some orange paint in the same way. Apply to the frame with a clean sponge on top of the blue paint, using the same circular motion. Allow the orange paint to dry.

3. To give the mount a more finished look, take a fine brush and paint the inner bevelled edge of the mount with blue paint. Use unthinned paint for an even coverage, and try to keep your hand steady as you go.

WATER COLOUR LINES

T his technique can take a little practice to perfect, but once mastered, you can use it in a variety of ways by the addition of extra lines to create an interesting border around a picture. It is always advisable to mark out the positions of your lines before you begin, using a pencil and ruler, to help guide you and prevent mistakes. Wet the board between the pencil lines using clean water before you start painting, and select a brush the same width as your border, if possible. We then edged the water colour line with silver pen to cover any uneven edges and make a smart finish.

You can obviously change the colours to suit your picture, but if you find it difficult to achieve an even colour, try using coloured pencils or crayons instead. The silver pen can always be replaced with black or gold, or even a coloured fibre-tipped pen in any shade you like.

The more proficient you become, the more adventurous you can be with your design. You will find that many different pieces of artwork can be enhanced by the use of these lines on the mount.

1. Lightly mark out the positions for the lines using a pencil and ruler. Take great care to make your measurements accurate: any discrepancy will show up clearly, especially when the mount is in the frame.

2. Use a fine artist's brush to dampen the area between the lines which you intend to paint. Then apply water colour to the same area, painting very carefully up to the lines. You will need a fine brush and a steady hand.

3. Once the paint is dry, draw over the pencil lines with a silver pen and ruler. We also added a silver spot at each corner (useful for disguising messy joins) and silver spots on top of the blue paint as decoration.

TROMPE L'OEIL STONES

Trompe l'oeil is a decorative technique which has been used in interior design for centuries. The words literally mean 'deceive the eye', which in this case is making the mountboard look like it is made from stone. I have also used a double thickness of mountboard to create a more chunky bevelled edge to add to the deception. The two layers are cut together and when placed one on top of the other, you can hardly see the join on the bevelled edge. The two pieces do not need to be glued together; you will find they will stay in place.

Creating the actual stone effect does not take a great deal of skill. The base colours, two shades of beige, are applied with a sponge in a fairly random fashion and the edges of the stones are painted on afterwards. The only time-consuming part is measuring out the edges of the individual stones and it is important to get this right so that the wall looks convincing. It is best to use a ruler to paint the lines to get a straight edge, but do use it upside down so the bevelled nature of the ruler holds the sides off the mountboard.

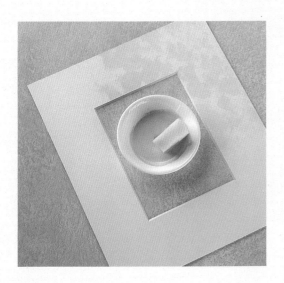

1. Mix white and brown acrylic with water to make a light beige base. Wet a sponge and dip in the paint, then remove any excess on scrap paper. Lightly sponge the colour on the mount, leaving bare areas showing. Reserve the unused paint.

2. Mix a darker beige, using more brown paint than before. Sponge the mount in the same way, lightly blending the colours and smoothing out sharp lines. Then sponge on a little more light beige, this time very sparingly. Reserve both colours.

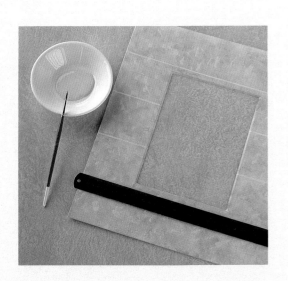

3. When the paint is dry, mark on the edges of the stones lightly with pencil and ruler. Take a fine artist's brush and paint along the pencil lines with the light beige paint, using the ruler to guide you. Don't worry if the lines are uneven.

4. Use the darker beige to paint along beside the light beige lines, making sure you don't cover them. Make sure the darker lines are always on the same side of the lighter lines; for example, below and to the left.

TARTAN MOUNT

A tartan mount can look very interesting, but because it is such a bold pattern, it does need to be used carefully. It can, however, look stunning in the right context. For example, it could create a rather unusual feel if used with botanical prints and look equally attractive if used with more 'masculine' types of work like old maps or architectural prints.

The mount is simply covered in tartan paper, so there is no creative skill needed at all to make this mount. There are many different tartan papers available, from the well-known patterns such as Royal Stewart to the unusual tartans such as the burgundy MacGregor.

The principle of covering a mount does not have to be restricted to tartan paper. There is a huge range of different giftwrapping papers now available which could be suitable for this project. Even wallpaper could be used, as long as it is not too stiff.

Always use a second mount within the paper-covered mount to create a plain border around the artwork. This is especially important if the paper is highly patterned. It will serve to establish a firm perimeter and stop the pattern from becoming too overbearing.

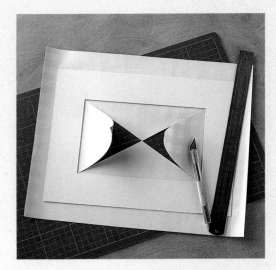

1. Cut an inner mount from coloured board. Cut an outer mount, which is to be covered in paper, making the window larger than that on the first mount. Stick double-sided tape on the outer mount, and cut a rectangle of paper to cover it.

2. Remove the backing paper from the tape and stick the mount squarely on the back of the paper. Cut two diagonal lines across the paper in the inner window to create four flaps using a ruler and sharp knife. Trim off the excess paper.

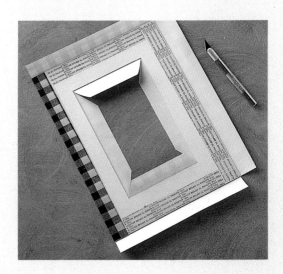

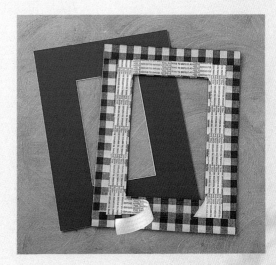

3. Remove a neat square of paper from each of the outer corners as shown. Stick tape along all inner and outer edges of the back of the mount, remove the backing paper and fold all flaps over on to it, creasing along each edge carefully.

4. Stick double-sided tape around all sides of the back of the tartan mount. Lay the inner, coloured mount face up on a firm surface. Remove the backing paper from the tape and lower the tartan mount on top of the other, aligning it perfectly.

PETAL MOUNT

There is a wide variety of handmade papers on the market with an interesting texture than cannot be found in manufactured papers. The uneven and natural look can enhance many framed pictures, and as handmade papers are usually available in a good range of colours, you should find one to suit your requirements. The use of pressed petals to enhance the mount adds to the naturalness and can look very pretty.

Pressing flowers is not difficult and you do not need a flower press to do it. Take the flowers and gently lay them on a double layer of tissue paper. Cover with another double layer of tissue, making sure the petals do not fold. Place the tissue bundle between the pages of a heavy book and pile extra books on top to increase the weight. The flowers will take between two and four weeks to press, depending on their thickness. Be careful when you remove them as they can be quite brittle; you may find a pair of tweezers helps when handling them. As an alternative, you could use pressed leaves if you feel they would be more suitable. These can be successfully pressed in exactly the same way.

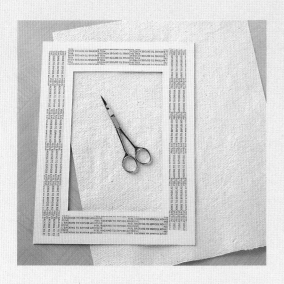

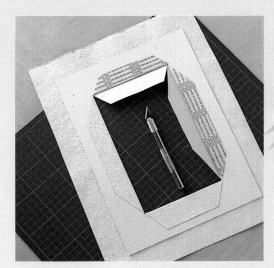

1. Cut a piece of handmade paper slightly larger than the mount to allow extra for turning. Stick double-sided tape to the front of the mount and remove the backing paper. Lay the mount face down in the centre of the paper and press firmly.

2. Stick double-sided tape around the inner edge of the back of the mount. Using a craft knife, cut the paper in the window from corner to corner across the diagonal. Cut off the excess paper and fold the tabs over, pressing firmly to stick in place.

3. Stick tape along the outer edge of two opposite sides of the mount. Cut away the corners of the paper and fold over the two opposite sides, sticking them firmly into place. Stick down the other two sides in the same way.

4. Pull the petals from the pressed flowers using a pair of tweezers. Use a cocktail stick to apply spots of glue to the backs of the petals and press into place on the mount. Thin PVA glue with water and paint over the petals to seal them.

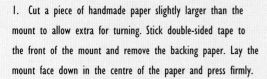

117

RIBBON DECORATION

A coloured line or border surrounding a picture will often enhance it. If a colour is chosen from the picture to make a line or border, it will bring that colour out in the picture, making it more prominent. In addition, the line itself can create an inner boundary which can give the picture more importance. This effect could be achieved by use of a double mount, but an alternative method is to use lines of ribbon glued onto the mountboard.

The advantage of using ribbon is that you do not need to worry about creating a line of even colour, nor do you need to worry about getting the lines straight, as long as your initial measurements are correct. Also, you have the opportunity of using a variety of decorative ribbons, such as those with wavy edges, to create effects that would not be possible without a great deal of artistic skill if you used paint or paper.

There is a wonderful range of ribbons available now, and most at very reasonable prices, especially as you need so little to decorate a mount. You can choose from such a wide range of colours, widths, patterns, textures and surface finishes, that you are sure to get just what you want.

1. Cut an inner and outer mount using a sharp knife. Use a pencil and ruler to mark where the ribbon will go on the outer mount. Draw lines where the inner edges of the ribbon should go, extending them by the width of the ribbon at both ends.

2. Measure the length of each line and cut pieces of ribbon to fit. Spread a line of glue, the width of the ribbon, above the top pencil line and below the bottom one. Stick the top and bottom ribbons in position, pulling them taut and straight.

3. Cut the ends of the pieces of ribbon for the two sides diagonally at 45° using sharp scissors. Spread glue on the outside of the pencil lines as before and stick the remaining ribbons in place. The angled ends will form mitred corners.

SPECKLED MOUNT

The technique for making these speckled mounts is the same as that used for the Spattered Granite frame on page 46. The only difference is that here the spattered effect has been softened by flicking the paint onto wet varnish. The effect can be as subtle or as bold as you wish depending on how much paint you spatter and the colours you choose. We have used two different colours to deepen the finish, but you could use more or fewer as you like. Perhaps you could choose one or more colours from your picture to make a completely co-ordinated look.

Spattering is not difficult, though it is a good idea to practise your technique on a piece of scrap paper first. If you use an artist's brush, as we have, it is best to strike the handle against a hard surface such as the handle of a wooden spoon. You could also use a toothbrush to create a similar effect, by drawing your finger over the bristles to flick the paint. You will get slightly different effects with different brushes, so try out a few before you begin.

1. Lay the mount on a flat surface, slightly raised above it, and apply a good, even coat of varnish. While the varnish is still wet, mix some raw sienna oil paint with a little white spirit to thin it down.

2. Load a paint brush with the thinned paint, not too much, and strike the handle of the brush against the handle of a wooden spoon to spatter the paint on the mount. Remove any very large spots of paint with white spirit-soaked tissue.

3. Repeat the spattering process with paint of a different colour: we chose a rich green. While the varnish is still wet, apply dabs of both colours to the mount with a fine artist's brush to add interest. Then paint the inner bevelled edge in green.

LAYERED TISSUE

The best thing about this idea is that you can use the same technique to create your own patterns with your own mix of colours to make a totally unique mount tailor-made for a picture or piece of artwork. It can be as vibrant as the ones we have made here, or you could make a more subtle version using very pale tissue papers and reducing the number of strips you use. You could move away from the checked effect and just have random patches of different tissues in similar colours for a very soft finish.

Another good point about this mount is that it doesn't need a bevelled inner edge because you are covering it with tissue. You can, therefore, cut the whole thing out with a craft knife.

If you do use brightly-coloured tissue on your mount, be careful as the colour does have a tendency to run when it is wet. That is why it is important to seal the mount on both sides when it is finished using a coat of thinned PVA glue. This will prevent the colour bleeding onto your picture. Make sure the glue you use is acid-free or it may affect the picture.

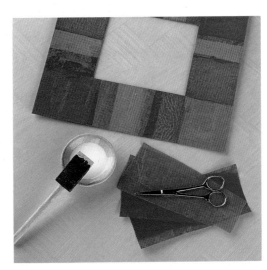

1. Cut two squares of each colour tissue slightly larger than the corners of your mount. Paint thinned PVA glue over the mount corners and lay the tissue paper on top. Cut the tissue corners as shown and glue the excess onto the back of the mount.

2. Cut strips of tissue in differing widths and glue them on the mount as shown, sticking the ends on the back of the mount. For best effect, alternate the colours and overlap the strips to create another colour band where the two meet.

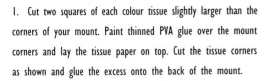

3. Cut some long thin strips in each colour and glue down the centre of each side to create a check effect. Extra strips can be glued to any wide bands of colour to balance the pattern. Glue any loose ends onto the back of the mount.

4. Once the glue has dried, paint the entire mount with a coat of thinned PVA glue to seal it. Paint both the front and back of the mount to seal the loose edges. The glue will dry clear to give the delicate tissue paper a tough, protective finish.

GOLD STAR MOUNT

Using a double mount can extend the variety of colours that could be chosen to complement a picture. For example, a strongly-coloured mount could look too powerful as it stands, but if doubled up with a mount in a more neutral shade so that it just creates an inner border, it could have a very pleasing effect.

This mount makes use of plain white mountboard. which is painted in yellow and gold to create the desired effect. Gold, in particular, is a versatile colour which lends itself well as a partner to many other shades, but it has been used extensively in picture framing in the past. However, with the yellow sponged paint finish and the addition of gold stars, a more contemporary feel is created. If you don't like stars, you could use spots instead, or you could even add a pattern to the inner mount to create more of a definite border.

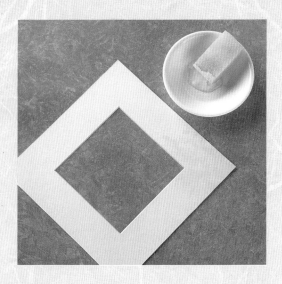

1. Cut two mounts, the inner with a smaller window than the outer. Dip a damp sponge into yellow acrylic paint, dab the excess off on a piece of scrap paper, then sponge onto the top mount, applying random patches to create a mottled effect.

2. When the paint is thoroughly dry, draw small stars onto the mount over the yellow paint using a gold fibre-tip pen. Keep the pattern of stars fairly random to achieve the most natural look. Allow the ink to dry before handling.

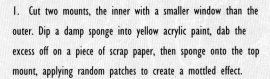

3. Paint the inner mount using gold acrylic paint, taking care not to paint over the bevelled edge along the inside of the mount. You only need to paint the section that will show when the two mounts are placed together. Allow to dry.

4. Stick double-sided tape around the inner edge of the back of the yellow mount and remove the backing paper. Lay the gold inner mount on a flat surface and position the yellow mount on top, aligning them carefully before pressing together.

STRIPED MOUNT

This stylish, striped inner mount can be used where you want a subtle, graphic decoration between the picture and the mount proper. It looks most effective when used in conjunction with a mount of a deep colour, like the black and rich red ones we have used here. We have used black stripes on both mounts for a very smart feel, but you could use any colour you choose, perhaps also varying the colour of the inner mountboard.

Instead of using stripes, you could use other patterns such as wavy lines, spots, stars or squares, either maintaining the graphic approach or creating a more casual appearance. The pattern chosen could reflect some part of the picture you are framing to extend the total image to cover the mount too.

If you do not feel confident enough to paint onto the inner mount, you may consider covering it with a patterned paper, in the same way as the Tartan Mount on page 114. The effect would be different from that of water colour, but you would still have a patterned inner mount for your picture.

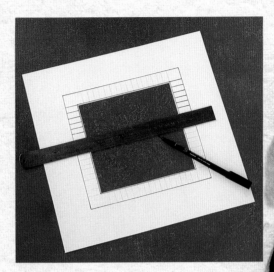

1. Cut two mounts, the inner with a smaller window than the outer. Draw a pencil line around the window of the inner mount, outside the area that will be visible when the two mounts are assembled. Measure out and draw the stripes.

2. When you are happy with the arrangement of stripes, use a fine, fibre-tipped pen to draw over the pencil lines, including the line around the inner edge of the stripes. It will be easier to draw the edge first and draw the stripes up to it.

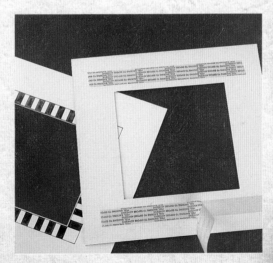

3. Use water colour and a fine artist's brush to fill in the stripes, aiming for an even coverage. Don't dilute the paint too much or it will overwet the board and cause the surface to warp as it dries. Take care not to paint outside the pen lines.

4. Stick double-sided tape onto the back of the top mount and remove the backing paper. Lay the inner mount on a firm surface and lower the top mount onto it, aligning the edges carefully before you press the two firmly together.

INDEX